BIBLICAL SEXUALITY

AND

THE BATTLE FOR SCIENCE

F. Earle Fox

All Scripture quotations are
from the Revised Standard Version
unless otherwise noted.

Emmaus Ministries
25 Parallel St.
Norwalk, Connecticut 06850

Copyright 1988, F. Earle Fox

Printed in the U. S. A.
by Ripon Community Printers
Ripon, Wisconsin

Library of Congress Card Catalogue Number: 88-80409

ISBN Number: 0-945778-00-7

Table of Contents

To the Glory of God

and the

Return of the King

Introduction

The Episcopal Church is the venue for the debate in which these articles participate, but the issues span the length and breadth of Christendom. The ability of the Christian community to understand and counter the inroads of secularism into the innermost halls of the Church has to be a matter of highest priority. It is my hope that these contributions will help establish a solid ground upon which the Church in the modern world can stand to make a clear, consistent, and realistic witness to the person and good news of Jesus Christ.

The first two articles included in this book were written in 1987 in response to two items published by diocesan commissions in the Episcopal Church on the matter of changing sexual morality. The third resulted from an encounter with the sexology of Alfred Kinsey.

The extraordinary demolition of the moral position which had been part of the fabric of western civilization for nearly two millenia, to all appearances within just three decades, is no small matter and one which demands an explanation. The Judeo-Christian framework out of which western morality has emerged is no longer one in which western civilization finds its identity or has any confidance. Even within the Christian and Jewish communities there has for decades been clear evidence of our roots in deep and stable tradition having atrophied seemingly beyond the point of possible healing.

It has not been so much that a superior religion has replaced the Biblical one, but rather that a strange erosion has occurred in our ability to deal with the ultimate questions of truth and life. This has been accompanied by, and abetted by, a growing sense that, on one hand, we *can* make it on our own without God, and on the other hand, that we are *condemned* to making it on our own. Emerging parallel with the growing confidence in man's ability to manage his own affairs without God has been a deepening sense of a terrible abyss opening up, that the very fabric of life was crumbling, that meaning and direction and purpose were a thing of the past, never to be recovered because we have come to the truth of life, that God, the source of meaning and purpose, was dead. The smarter we got technologically and scientifically, the dimmer the prospects seemed to be for an ultimately meaningful life. The "tragic sense of life" which has run through so much art and literature of all cultures seemed to have a clear scientific foundation.

I have never had any trouble dealing with the philosophical issues involved in these events, or in maintaining my own intellectual integrity as a Christian, to my satisfaction at least, in the face of massive cultural disagreement. It puzzled me, even as a child, that so many "bought the balony" of the secular worldview. I could not understand what was behind so many being persuaded that God did not exist, or that if He once did, He had, somewhere in the last century or so, died.

Most of my life has been spent "thinking", proving to myself and anyone else who would listen that the "God answer" was the only logical and rational answer to the questions of life. But ideas, as powerful as they may be, are just ideas. Somewhere the rubber, as they say, has to hit the road. It has to make a difference in how we behave and relate to one another. Ideas have to mesh gears with will and action. And one cannot merely counter bad ideas, one has to find the actual physical, cultural point at which evil ideas are taking effect.

While all this proving was going on in my own mind, the culture around me was continuing to erode and disintegrate. "Statistics" continued to get worse with little prospect of improving. And right in the middle of the mess was the downward spin into sexual permissiveness and choas. And the same question: Why is this happening? What or who is causing this? The so-called "new morality" clearly, to me at least, made no sense, no common sense, no philosophical sense, and so far as I knew, no scientific sense. Having been a clergyman and pastoral counselor for the three decades of the precipitous decline, I felt I had some hands-on knowledge of the issues. I have seen children grow up in the most promising way, and then watched them be destroyed before my eyes as they hit the peer culture of the teen years. The blame cannot be laid at the door of teen culture alone, but there is clearly something terrible that is eating children up during those years.

2

I do not have any doubt that Satan exists and that he or his minions were intimately involved in such cases. But evil, like good, also uses human resources, human institutions, human commitment to get its way. And while there seemed to be many institutions and persons and philosophies that one could point to as being off the track of truth and righteousness (naziism, communism, etc.) yet none of them seemed to be the <u>cause</u> of what was happening around us. And of course, there is not likely to be any one cause.

But occasionally one stumbles on an identifiable primary source, a tap root leading down into a cesspool of evil, that is feeding death into the bloodstream of culture and civilization. These three articles document my own experience of stumbling onto what appears to me to be such a source.

The source is not itself within the Church, but the streams of its lethal flow have meandered quite nonchalantly among us, and we have, to our great distress and confusion, and now increasingly death, drunk deeply.

None of this could have happened had the Church not lost its own sense of identity in the Biblical framework, the Biblical cosmos, and the Biblical God and Father of the cosmos. None of this could have happened had the Church had a healthy relationship to the scientific community. Had we been rooted in the truth in a healthy way, we would have spotted this poison, named it for what it was, and thrown it out of our midst.

But, as the first two articles indicate, that did not happen. We remain, with noteable exceptions, in a state of indecision, impotence, paralysis and pseudo-pastoral stance while people are physically and emotionally and spiritually dying all around us. If the perceptions which I share below are true, the Church in its present state is of only mediocre assistance to the Kingdom of God, and not much threat to the kingdom of Satan, being not able even clearly to distinguish between the two.

My high school english teacher used to insist that we "go to the source material". And I recommend the reader to likewise. Do not take my word for anything said. Follow up with investigation of your own. Visit your school system and insist on seeing the sex education materials (they are not

3

necessarily all bad, but you might be amazed).
Visit your local Planned Parenthood office and discover what their philosophy of sexual morality is.
Read through a copy of *Playboy* or *Hustler*, or visit
your local "adult" bookshop. Go to the library and
read Kinsey's work on human sexuality. Then ask
yourself if you see a common thread running through
these experiences.

And pray and read your Bible (better do that
first, you will need preparation). And then you
decide. And then act.

I.

SEXUALITY AND FAMILY LIFE

THE BIBLICAL ROOTS

Part I -- BIBLICAL OR "PERENNIAL"?

A. Clearing Our Vision

"Some disasters have to be seen to be believed."
The words caught my eye in a letter to the editor
of one of the Episcopal Church magazines some eight
or ten years ago describing a book called THE SEX
ATLAS which was put out by Seabury Press, then the
Episcopal Church publishing house. I could hardly
believe my eyes. The book was alleged to give a
scientific, moral, and religious approval to such
sexual niceties as pre-marital sex, incest, and
bestiality. The Episcopal Church had committed
some blunders in its history, but this was quite
literally beyond belief. So I spent the 18 or so
dollars to obtain this gem, which turned out in
plain fact to be a massive, several hundred pages
of the most explicit photographic and textual de-
scriptions and approval of the sort of sexual behavior mentioned in the letter.

I wrote to the publisher. I wrote to the diocesan headquarters. I wrote to the magazine in question. I wrote to the Presiding Bishop at national
headquarters. What I thought would be a thunderous
explosion was an hardly audible, "We do not want to
embarrass the Church", and "Do not worry, it will
be seen to." And then I heard no more. Later I
brought the matter to the attention of the local
clergy and lay leaders at our deanery meeting.
Having since burned my edition, seeing it had no
practical use, I offered to get a new copy as few
at the meeting believed my report. Only a small
handful were interested in pursuing the truth of
the matter. So it was tabled by default.

5

Recently the Episcopal Diocese of Newark, New Jersey, published a paper entitled, "Report of the Task Force on Changing Patterns of Sexuality and Family Life" (see copy attached). The report does not give approval to either bestiality or incest. It does, however, maintain that sex outside of marriage and homosexual unions ought under certain circumstances (apparently to be subjectively decided by the persons involved themselves since objective standards are all but demolished) to be blessed by the Church. The Newark report does not go as far as the SEX ATLAS, but it is difficult to see what would prevent that from happening, given the presuppositions from which the report appears to have been written.

The Presiding Bishop of the Episcopal Church, Edmond Browning, is reported in *The Episcopalian* as follows:

> His seventh imperative for the Church's mission is to "support individuals and families in their struggles for wholeness." He warned, however, "we must move beyond the middle-class smugness of focusing on the Dick-and-Jane families of the 1950's and start dealing with the realities of family life today!" He said he finds "my wholeness in marriage" but can also "walk in faith" with those who have made other choices. Many will refuse to hear his message, he said, but "it is my firm belief and my vision for this Church that we will acknowledge that God works within each of us to make and keep us whole."[1]

The uncomplementary reference to "Dick-and-Jane families" and the affirmation to "walk in faith with those who have made other choices", presumeably to find their sexual expression outside of family life, appear to point in a direction far afield from the Biblical viewpoint. Is the "reality of family life today" the fact that many persons are choosing openly to express genital sexuality apart from heterosexual marriage? No one would contend that God does not work to make each of us whole, or that we are to walk in love with those of other choices, but Biblical witness contends that

---

1 November, 1987, page 14. Bishop Browning had given eight "mission imperatives", opening up the first plenary session of the meeting of the House of Bishops at Chicago, September 27 to October 1. This was the seventh. The eighth is referred to below, Part II, Section D, "Pluralism, Inclusiveness, and Relative Truth".

God does not approve of all those ways we so often seek to make ourselves whole. We are also required to walk in truth and obedience.

Some disasters have to be seen to be believed. But the greater disaster is when the disaster stares us back in the face, and we think we have discovered it to be a "profound new truth" about life. My Old Testament professor at General Seminary said once that sin was not "crouching" at Cain's door (Genesis 4:7) as in some translations, but "couching". If it had been crouching, like a lion ready to spring and devour, it would have been recognised as an enemy. But it was couching, lying comfortably at the fireside like a family pet. This disaster that has to be seen to be believed lies couching at the fireside not only of western civilization, but of many of our churches. And we do not believe it because we in truth do not see it.

I used to listen to this "new way" of expressing the Christian faith and think to myself, "They really are saying the same thing that I believe, it just *sounds* different because they are trying to reach out to modern folks." Finally it dawned on me that this is *not* the same Gospel in different dress, it is a *fundamentally* contrary "Good News" which is neither good nor new. We are staring at the same basic enemy of the Gospel confronted by the Hebrews and Christians in the pagan spirituality and philosophies of Egypt, Canaan, Babylon, and Rome. The only thing new is the sophisticated aura of modern and increasingly bankrupt secular materialism.

In fairness it must be said that it would probably be difficult for anyone raised in the 20th century western culture to see the disaster, precisely because the mindset that governs that culture *is* the disaster. When you are raised immersed in a particular mindset, it is very difficult to step aside and observe it objectively. Anyone raised in the west in the last 400 years is partially a child of secular materialism. Most Christians today are struggling within themselves to paste a Gospel message over an underlying secular view of life. We are deeply in need of a thorough brain-washing, a scrubbing with the Holy Spirit brillo pad to bring us back to an authentic Biblical view and experience of the cosmos.

I would not have bothered even to mention the absurd situation of THE SEX ATLAS had it not become glaringly apparant again that the more basic issue is still very much with us. Lest one think that this kind of nonsense happens only in big and un-read tomes and in ultra-liberal theological cir-cles, consider the following from the May 5, 1987 edition of the WESTPORT NEWS from my neighboring town of Westport, Connecticut, concerning a text-book used in the public school system for sex edu-cation, entitled LEARNING ABOUT SEX -- A CONTEMPO-RARY GUIDE FOR YOUNG ADULTS, by Gary F. Kelly:

> After describing in full detail foreplay, mutual masturbation, sexual intercourse, in our opinion, the text book author suggests that children should try oral sex and anal sex. Mr. Kelly tells them how it is done on page 70-71: (Editor's note: The Kraus-es included here from the texbook a graphic, specif-ic description of anal sex. We have omitted it.)

> Mr. Kelly says: "There are no indications that such animal contacts (intercourse) are harmful, ex-cept for the obvious dangers of poor hygiene, injury by the animal or to the animal, or guilt on the part of the human." (Page 61)

The disaster is couching at our door.

And yet, as grotesque as the sexual aberations of our time indeed are, they are not the basic issue. The deeper issue is rather the spiritual warfare behind the scenes represented by two mor-tally opposed worldviews. It is that opposition of worldviews that I wish to discuss -- in the context of the "Report of the Task Force on Changing Pat-terns of Sexuality and Family Life" issued by the Episcopal Diocese of Newark, a report which is only a hop, skip, and a jump from the morality of THE SEX ATLAS.

I say that sexual behavior is not the deepest issue, but it is nevertheless true that the spiri-tual warfare between Christ and the world can be put in sexual and gender terms at its deepest lev-els. It is the expression of these two views in their sexuality that we are dealing with on a mas-sive cultural scale today. If we are going to dis-cern what is the mind of God on issues of sexuality such as those raised by the report from the Diocese of Newark, we must have a reasonbly clear notion of what is Biblical and what is not. Policies that are a contradiction to the general Biblical framework will not fare well as candidates for representing the will of God. Those that are consistent with the Biblical view have at least a running chance.

B. The "Perennial" View

Aldous Huxley, an English philosopher, some years ago wrote a book entitled THE PERENNIAL PHILOSOPHY in which he maintained that there is really only one way of looking at life. He called it the "perennial" philosophy because, he says, it crops up in every culture known to man quite apart from historical contact.[2] John DeVries, the leader of the missionary enterprise, "Bibles for India", describes what he calls the "Hindu mindset", which he says, has already deeply infiltrated the American scene. America, he says, is no longer a Biblically oriented nation. America has become in its mindset a Hindu nation.[3]

The Hindu worldview described by DeVries is none other than the Perennial Philosophy of Huxley. DeVries is philosophically right on target excepting that one need not go to Hinduism to find the mindset to which he points. One need only step outside of the Biblical worldview (into the so-called "New Age" movement, for example) to find himself drifting very decidedly in that direction. But Huxley was wrong. There are *two* basic ways of looking at the cosmos, not just one, the Biblical way and the Perennial way. Contrary to Huxley and others of his persuasion, there simply is no way that the Biblical worldview can be adapted to fit into the Perennial way. Whichever one is true, the other of logical necessity must be false. Furthermore, one finds the same underlying pattern of this Perennial view whether one drifts into modern secular materialism or into the more mysterious and esoteric reaches of oriental Hinduism or any of the other eastern religions.

---

2 Huxley, Aldous, THE PERENNIAL PHILOSOPHY, Fontana 1958, London.

3 John DeVries describes this Hindu mindset very clearly in a cassette tape, "Eastern Religions in the West", available from Bibles for India, 4221 Richmond St., N. W., Grand Rapids, MI 49504. The four points he gives are included in the description I am offering.

We can give here only a very brief description
of the basic and irresolveable antagonism between
the Biblical and Perennial views, but other more
fully developed resources are available.[4]   A
part of the baggage of our pluralistic culture is
that within the Church itself it has become a matter of great speculation as to what in fact quali-
fies as "Biblical". On the one hand, we have bene-
fited greatly from the scientific exploration of
the Bible through literary, anthropological, and
other techniques, and have now a rather large common fund of agreed upon knowledge concerning the
Bible which has brought Christians together across
many and varied denominational lines. But on the
other hand we have not resolved some very basic
philosophical and theological questions as to what
"Biblical" means, and so the same Bible continues
to be used by both sides of warring parties within
the Church. These divisions are again about to
rend the Church apart. It is vital that clear
standards be found for deciding what is in fact
Biblical and what is not.

It is my contention that a fairly straight forward reading of the Bible will discover, once one
knows what to look for, a cosmic and philosophical
framework unique to the Bible which far outclasses
anything secular or pagan philosophy can give us.
The intellectually defensive attitude and the cultural inferiority complex under which Christians

---

4 I have described on audio cassette tape these two views in detail, showing the
  evolving of the nature of the perennial view out of its primitive origins into what
  we know as materialism or humanism and its sister eastern spiritualism. These
  tapes (numbers A-1.1 and A-1.2) are available from Emmaus Ministries (see final
  note for further information). The cassettes run for approximately two hours each.
  We hope to have the same material on video cassette by the fall of 1987.
      Another superb resource is the work of Stanley Jaki, who has written extensive-
  ly and very deeply on the relation between science and religion, and who is one of
  the very few writers who has picked up on the clear distinction between the pagan
  and Biblical worldviews. See especially SCIENCE AND CREATION, Scottish Academic
  Press 1974, Edinburgh. Also relevant are COSMOS AND CREATOR (Gateway 1980, Chicago) and THE ROAD OF SCIENCE AND THE WAYS TO GOD (University of Chicago 1978,
  Chicago). Jaki is not light reading, but well worth the effort if one is interested in well documented and well grounded arguments.
      Also of value is a group called "Spiritual Counterfeits Project", which spe-
  cializes in research to distinguish between authentically Biblical and non-Biblical
  religions and other groups. Their intellectual integrity is excellent as they do
  their research homework before making statements concerning any group. They may be
  contacted at PO Box 4308, Berkeley, CA 94704. Materials are available for free or
  at minimal charge on most of the cults, religions, and movements current today.

have labored for at least three centuries since the rise of secular humanism is totally unnecessary.[5] But this truth needs to be drawn out in clear terms so that Christians can present this truth in a manner that commands attention from any willing listener. The spiritual warfare in which we are engaged is not at all wholly academic or intellectual or philosophical, but the academic *is an essential part* of the battle. If our homework is not done in that area, then we will always appear out of touch with realilty to others and labor under a niggling sense of inferiority within ourselves. If we do not have a clear notion of what the Biblical worldview is in the first place and a confidance that it is real, we will continue to labor under the difficulty of trying to paste a Gospel message on top of an essentially pagan and materialist worldview.

Lest this appear an overly academic essay, let me underline that we are engaged in spiritual warfare, not polite "merely academic" discussion. Merely presenting the truth rationally will not win many for Christ. But we must nevertheless present the truth as clearly and rationally as we can. When God warned Adam about the dangers before him, He said nothing at all about Satan or a serpent lurking in the Garden. He said merely, "Do not eat of the Tree of the Knowledge of Good and Evil." Had Satan been the one to worry about, God would have warned Adam. But Satan was not the point of danger.

The Tree of the Knowledge of Good and Evil is a symbol common in ancient mythology. A tree had often been taken as a symbol of the cosmos, no doubt due to the sense of the depth of the roots beneath and the overarching branches above with the "living space" in between. There are such symbolic trees in Hindu and in Scandinavian lore as well as others. But these trees do not represent just any old cosmos. They represent the cosmos as a self-contained and self-sufficient entity, responsible to no God beyond itself. The danger of which

---

5 I owe much of what I am saying to one college professor, Edmund Cherbonnier, at whose feet I sat at Trinity College, Hartford, Connecticut in the 1950's. He taught, and convinced me of the truth, that the Bible has the only logically consistent and philosophically respectible philosophy that there is, and that Huxley's Perennial Philosophy is disasterously lacking in philosophical integrity. Both Jaki and DeVries mentioned in the above footnotes, as well as many others, have picked up on some of the same truths.

God was warning Adam was the danger of thinking that he lived or desiring that he might live in such a cosmos and that he, Adam, might himself be or become one day self-sufficient, a thought that lurks within each of us. Seeking nurture from the forbidden tree was a rejection of our dependency on God. The death of which God warned was the inevitable and natural consequence of an inherently dependent being trying to live as though he were self-sufficient. The reason Satan was not mentioned in the warning was that Satan was no threat to those who lived their lives in a total dependency on the Creator, the state of Adam and Eve in the Garden before the Fall.

The *primary and basic characteristic* of the pagan worldview, then, is that there is no ultimate personal Creator upon which the cosmos is dependent and to whom it is responsible. The cosmos is itself the eternal and divine entity, the "Great Mother" of ancient pagan religion, the original, primal and self-sufficient Source of all that is. One might define paganism as the belief that there is no distinction between God and the cosmos. To be in touch with nature or the cosmos *is* to be in touch with God. The same is true of modern secular materialism or secular humanism. The basic enduring entity is nature itself, the cosmos. And although materialists would not talk about a personal God, the cosmos functions in crucial respects as being the eternal and reliable and basic stuff of life upon which we all depend for our meaning and welfare. As Carl Sagan tells us in his COSMOS series, we are made of "star stuff", the original cosmic soup out of which all things emerged.

The *second distinguishing characteristic* of the Perennial way is that there is in the final analysis no objective truth. Truth is relative. Whatever one affirms of ultimate reality must also be denied, since ultimate reality contains everything that is, and since both good and evil (for example) exist, ultimate reality must contain them both without preference. Reality is therefore irreducibly ambiguous at the core of its being. There is no truth for which we do not also have to make room for its opposite. This becomes especially apparent in moral and spiritual issues. The contemporary version of this is our so-called "pluralistic society" in which we are persuaded to harbor wildly opposing views to avoid being "judgemental". "Pluralism" is treated as a virtue when it is in fact an unfortunate (and hopefully passing) necessity. It is a sign of our disintegrating ability to agree on what the truth is.

This Perennial view is not one in which it is believed that there *is* an objective truth, but that we have some difficulty in discerning it and therefore need to be cautious about making pronoucements on it. Rather it is a view which says that there is no objective truth to begin with, and therefore claiming truth for one's particular viewpoint is a denial of rights to those who hold a contrary viewpoint. As in the Dodo bird's Caucus Race (Alice in Wonderland), everybody wins and everybody gets a prize. We all have a right to our viewpoint without being held responsible for establishing whether it is true or false. That, of course, follows naturally if there is no ultimate and objective truth or falsehood. Most of our college campuses today teach truth on the "smorgosbord" theory: "Here are all the various and possible views of truth laid out on the table. Take which one fits your taste. If it works for you, then it *is* true *for you*." All truth is relative.

Allan Bloom begins THE CLOSING OF THE AMERICAN MIND:

> There is one thing a professor can be absolutely certain of: almost every student entering the university believes, or says he believes, that truth is relative.[6]

The following four hundred pages are a well written and devastating critique of the erosion of the academic community and of western culture due to our loss of a sense of objective truth.

The *third characteristic* of the Perennial mindset follows from the above. If there is no objective truth to begin with, then of course there can be no objective moral value either. All morality is relative. The Hindu scripture, BHAGAVAD-GITA, is one of the classical expressions of the viewpoint that morality and the meaning of life are essentially relative and more related to fate or chance than to reason. So morality, like truth, is something one chooses to suit his own private feelings on the matter. As there are no objective

---

6 Allan Bloom, THE CLOSING OF THE AMERICAN MIND, p. 25. Simon & Schuster, 1987. A book every Christian engaged in the battle with secularism should read.

standards, one is left with only the subjective and therefore easily changeable standards which one invents for him or herself.

The consequence of this is that there is no objective moral distinction between Abraham Lincoln, Ghandi, Ghengis Khan, Hitler, or Jesus. Since there is no behavior that is really right or really wrong, it follows that there are no people who can be called really right or wrong either, noble or ignoble, righteous or perverse. We are all simply "doing our own thing", just part of the cosmic flow of things, a neat solution to the problem of pain.

This then leads to the *fourth characteristic* that one finds the deepest level of life, the contact with the divine, essentially through feeling experience devoid of intellectual content. A great deal of eastern spirituality is geared specifically to divest our minds of any reliance on the intellect for its perception of ultimate reality, the specific aim, as for example of the Zen Buddhist koan, a concentration on nonsense sayings, or of Transcendental Meditation, a Hindu import. Again, it follows that if the ultimate reality is in essence ambiguous and unfathomable by the mind, if the mind can have no significant and true grasp of ultimate reality, then one must separate himself from dependency on the mind as an effective instrument to aid in approaching God. One must divest himself from reliance on logic and rational thinking. The result is, as we can see massively in our culture, a reliance on feelings and a loss of the sense of the objectivity of truth, spiritual and moral truth in particular, but a loss which is invading even that former bastion of objective truth, physics.[7]

Again, this is not merely a corrective, badly enough needed in western culture, to our over intellectualizing and overly analytical attitude. The Perennial view is not saying that we need to balance our intellectual approach to God with feelings and intuitive input. Rather it is saying that

---

7 See, for example, "A 'What You See Is What You Beget' Theory", DISCOVER, May 1987, p. 90 ff., which develops some of the contemporary implications of Einstein's theory of relativity and of the theory of indeterminacy. The drift is decidedly toward a subjective view of the whole cosmos, that is to say, solipsism.

For a popularized version of some of the physics involved, see Werner Heisenberg's, PHYSICS AND PHILOSOPHY, Harper and Bros., New York, 1958.

because the ultimate reality of life is itself by nature a "coincidence of opposites", an ambiguity, an uncertainty, therefore intellectual truth will always be untrue to life. There are no sure propositions that we can state about God and about our relationship with Him. Our supposed knowledge of God trails off into the infinite mists of obscurity.

It can be seen that each of these aspects of the Perennial view leads inexorably on to the next aspect. The *fifth characteristic* follows likewise from the previous four, namely that as one embarks on the spiritual journey to the divine, one is compulsively driven toward self-sufficiency and self-containment. The fact of one's dependent nature will be experienced as an affront. Our dependency will be seen as that which makes us vulnerable to "the slings and arrows of outrageous fortune," something to be avoided and overcome at all costs. Because there are no objective resources "out there" to establish one's sense of direction, meaning, and wellbeing, one is continually forced to establish them for himself. 'Autonomy' becomes the watchword.

C. The Biblical Picture

It does not take any great effort of observation to see that these characteristics have indeed become commonplace in contemporary western culture. These values saturate the media, our educational system (as in sex education), and indeed large areas of the Church. The New Age movement, the 1980's successor to the 1970's Age of Aquarius, is nothing new. It is simply another flowering of that same ancient and perennial root of the forbidden tree.

Whatever one thinks of the Bible, if one is honest he has to admit that it is saying something profoundly *different*. The Biblical cosmology contradicts the Perennial view on every one of the aboved listed points. (There are others as well, but these are sufficient for our purposes here.)

If the Biblical picture is the true one, then there is indeed a gap between God and the creation, not a chasm of the sort that separates us from relationship, but one rather which establishes our separate identities and indeed thereby makes relationship possible. God is not the creation, and the creation is not God. God, I AM, is quite able to be Himself with or without the creation. But *our* existence and identity is dependent on Him and upon our relationship to Him.

Furthermore, it is unquestioned in Scripture that there is a clear line between truth and untruth. There is an objective reality within which we have to live and to whom we are accountable. Elijah's words resound throughout Scripture, "How long will you go limping with two different opinions? If the Lord is God, follow Him; but if Baal, then follow him." (I Kings 18:21) This was followed by a put-your-money-where-your-mouth-is test to decide where the truth indeed lay.

The concept of relative truth is in most instances a mish-mash of poor thinking. Truth either is or is not. That is the basis of all rational thinking, the law of non-contradiction. That is why God named Himself "Yahweh" -- "I AM". The Old Testament notion of the jealous God is precisely this point, that there *is* only one God. If truth must indeed be relative, then let us have our relative truth, but it is relative to that being to whom it is responsible for its existence. Truth is relative to God who created it. It is *not* relative merely to itself or to our whims or preferences or to public opinion.

The intellect is therefore expected to play a significant part in our understanding of God and of His will for us. God is not trying to be mysterious or obscure, He is trying to be clear and precise. That, after all, is the basic presupposition of "revelation" in the first place. One does not reveal things by being cloudy and obscure, but by being clear and precise. God continually does things in our lives and then expects us to act reasonably in view of them. When a band of nobodies is freed through no virtue of their own from the mightiest power on earth, that is *good reason* to trust the Power that freed them. "Come, let us reason together...." echoes like a refrain (cf. Is.43:26). Nowhere in the Bible is reason as such ever cast in a bad light. It is in every case put

in a good light. Because the Hebrews were never
"professional philosophers" as were the Greeks it
is assumed that reason was not a part of their way
of life. The truth is that they in many areas
reasoned far better than any of the Greeks. But
they did not make a "god" of reason as did the
Greek (and many other) philosophers.

Thirdly, moral values likewise are objectively
given, not voted upon, not subjectively brought
into being, but given. God's purpose for existence
is the fundamental rock upon which all moral value
is grounded. [8]

And lastly, the Bible takes what from the
world's point of view is an intolerable deficit and
turns it into our glory. Our dependency becomes
our childhood to God, not that which makes us vulnerable to outrage, but precisely that which se-
cures our identity and our welfare and our viabili-
ty, right into eternity.

On every single basic issue, the Perennial view
of the forbidden Tree is not merely a few degrees
off course. It is 180 degrees contrary and diamet-
rically opposed to the view of the Bible. It is
that realm of which Jesus said Satan was the
"prince" (John 12:31). And it is into that realm
that we step when we part company with the view
given us of life and of the cosmos in the Hebrew
and Christian scriptures. It is indeed a "perennial". It springs up spontaneously wherever the Biblical plant has not taken firm root. The Perennial
view is one of the tares sown by the enemy in the
Lord's garden.

We are fighting, as Paul says, not against flesh
and blood but against principalities and powers.
It is not the believers in the Perennial way that
is the enemy. Them we must love. It is the spiritual power, partly represented by the false intellectual hold such a view has on such believers
against which we fight. No doubt some "perennial-
ists" will find themselves in front row seats in
heaven, not because of their "perennialism" but
because perhaps totally unknown to themselves they
fed Jesus, clothed Him, or visited Him in jail.
The enemy we are here discussing is the spiritual

_____
8 See my article, "Defining 'Oughtness' and 'Love'", JOURNAL OF RELIGION, July, 1959,
   p. 170 ff. The article gives the case to show that all objective morality depends
   on there being a purpose for existence and hence a Purposer for existence.
   Reprints available from Emmaus Ministries (see note at end of article).

power of the belief system. And the weapon is the sword of truth, used with intellectual integrity and decisiveness simply and solely to set ourselves and others free from falsehood.

D. Sex and Gender - Objective Standards

When God made us, He had a specific purpose for us to fulfill, namely to be sacraments of His glory. He decided to make us *in His image -- male and female*. The inescapable conclusion of Genesis 1:26-8 is that there was something already pre-existing in God of which Adam and Eve were to be the image or reflection or sacrament. There was something special in God of which Adam was the image, and something *different* but equally special in God of which Eve was the image. Since God is not a biological, physical being He was neither male nor female. But the spiritual qualities of masculinity and femininity can exist in God, and indeed it would be difficult to find any other candidates to fill the role. God is, in short, a fathering God and also a mothering God. These two roles can be clearly defined in Biblical language.[9]

It is a part of our materialist bias that we feel sexuality (the male-female, biological aspect) to be prior to gender (the masculine-feminine, spiritual aspect) of ourselves. When one asks the definition of 'masculinity', one is likely to get the response, 'behavior appropriate to a male'. The biological is thought of as prior to the spiritual or emotional or cultural. Freud has given us, or at least articulated for us, the legacy that genital sexual experience is the basic pleasure (and therefore the basic good) of all pleasures (and therefore of all goods). All other pleasure is in some way a substitute for, a sublimation of, genital sexual experience. Most westerners would probably not list that as a philosophically held item in their beliefs, but it is hard to get away from the impact of it nevertheless as it lies be-

---

9 I have outlined this gender distinction in God of which we are the image on cassette tapes available from Emmaus Ministries. A set of 12 tapes entitled, "A Theology of Sexuality", would be particularly helpful. See endnote on Emmaus Ministries for further information.

hind so much of media advertizing and entertainment, not to mention our warped notion of what passes for so-called "adult" literature.

The problem with the biological materialist approach is that it does not tell us what constitutes "appropriate" behavior for a male or a female. Cultures disagree widely on what they might consider masculine or feminine with the result that appropriateness is left to our personal and private definition. That is to say, it is a relative matter.

On the Biblical view, however, since gender, the spiritual aspect precedes the biological, sexual aspect, there is an objective standard by which "appropriate" behavior for males or females might be measured. The nature of God is already objectively there. Behavior which would be appropriate for males and females is therefore not a relative matter decided by culture or personal preference but grounded in the very nature of God. How that is specifically spelled out in Scripture is beyond the scope of this article.[10]

But the notion that the Bible is an inherently "patriarchal" book needs to be challenged. The Bible begins in a marriage, ends in a marriage, and right at the center is the Song of Solomon celebrating marital love. Sexual and gender imagery runs all through Scripture, most strikingly in the relation between God and His people. The Bible is a book about the union of masculine and feminine, male and female, not about their competition and incompatibility. The union is through distinction and complementarity, not by unisex merging and indistinguishability. The eternal battle of the sexes is a struggle inherent to the Perennial pattern, one of the attempted resolutions for which is unisex. Neither the built-in battle nor the unisex solution are a part of the Biblical view of sexuality or gender.

The relevant point however is that human kind are created to reflect the image and glory of God, and that that image and glory reflects gender relations which are an objective standard measuring the wholeness and completeness of what it means to be human. Being made in the image of God gives us an objective standard for human nature as a whole, not only for sexuality and gender, the Incarnation

---
10 Ibid.

being the final expression of that image in human terms. We are not cast into the sea of certain kinds of existentialism which maintain that there is no objective human nature and that we therefore have to create our own. We have a purpose and a direction given to us quite beyond our personal or corporate ability to determine, but which offers the deepest and richest life possible quite literally under any circumstances imaginable.

Assuming that this is a reasonably accurate description of the Bibical view of life as opposed to the Perennial view, we can proceed to review the report from the Diocese of Newark to assess whether in fact the recommendations of that report are acceptable within the Biblical framework.

Part II -- THE ISSUES

A. Our Changing Culture

The report issued by the Diocese of Newark addresses itself to three groups, "1) young people who choose to live together without being married; 2) older persons who choose not to marry or who may be divorced or widowed; 3) homosexual couples." (p. 1) The conclusion of the report is essentially that all three of these groupings of persons ought to be given fairly free reign to express their sexual preferences without interference from the Church, and indeed that the Church has been badly mistaken in not positively supporting them.

To support these conclusions, ten factors said to be characteristic of contemporary American culture are offered as reasons for altering "some of the basic moral values and assumptions which have long been taken for granted." (p. 2) It is said, seemingly with approval, that "today, the Church is no longer the single arbiter in these matters, which were once thought to be within its sacred province." (p. 2) The impression is that we have "come of age" and no longer need the Church in a parental role.

Each of the ten points given deserves much longer treatment than can be given here. I will be able to touch only briefly on each to indicate the manner in which the thrust of these ten points arises out of a prior viewpoint that is not revealed to present a case that only partially exists. And then we shall look at some of the presuppositions which appear to be behind the report.

(1) Secularization of American society as it moved from a predominately rural background at the turn of the century to today's predominately urban setting. This has produced new and competing centers of values and morality.

There is a hidden and unwarrented assumption that urbanization and/or technology itself produces the new and competing centers of values and morality with the corollary that traditional morality is linked to an outdated culture. The truth is that science and technology do not by themselves lead to a breakdown of Biblical morality, and it is misleading to suggest that they do. But they have been used by non-Biblical and anti-Biblical interests to make it appear to be the case. As Stanley Jaki and others have pointed out, science and techology are both historically and philosophically the product chiefly of an original Biblical foundation.[11] If there is a conflict between our technological society and the Christian faith, therefore, it will have to be found in some prior religious or philosophical stance of those opposing the Bible, not in the role of technology or science or urbanization itself. It is that prior stance we will be exploring.

(2) Social, economic and geographical mobility that has individually and collectively loosened structures traditionally provided by the community, church and family. These structures tended to channel and constrict values, choices, and behavior....

Mobility has indeed had some of the stated effect. But to say that these traditional structures "constricted" values etc., is to apply a loaded term and to beg the issue. The implication is that the constriction has been an unfair one, which is just the point at issue. There is an assumption that the present development of society is a good

---

11 See note above on Stanley Jaki. I have written a book, PERSONALITY, EMPIRICISM, AND GOD, which builds the case to show that the logic of science *requires* the Biblical creator God, which will be available in 1988 from Emmaus Ministries (see endnote).

one, that it is inevitable, and that therefore our thoughts about what God requires must bend to these cultural circumstances. The possibility that the culture may itself be destructive in its development, that development does not *ipso facto* imply *good* development, is not discussed.

(3) Advances of technology, which have provided means of disease control and birth control, which have effectively separated the act of sexual intercourse from procreation.

Again the assumption of a natural connection between technology and the "new" morality. Technology is itself morally neutral. The fact that a thing is possible tells us nothing about its goodness. It does not follow from the fact that we can separate intercourse from procreation that we should. (We can now also separate technology from the survival of the human race, but it does not follow that we should.) The question can be decided only on moral or spiritual ground which comes from outside of the technology of sex itself.

(4) Reduction of the age at which puberty begins. This confronts children with issues of sexuality earlier than in the past.

(5) Adolescent dating without chaperonage. This removes a powerful external structure of control of sexual behavior.

Puberty may begin earlier than previously, but that in itself tells us nothing at all about the quality of the morality that one might want to expect. Dating without chaperonage is treated as an accomplished and inevitable fact. The truth is that there are parents who still maintain a reasonable amount of control over the dating habits of their children. It is indeed more difficult to do so given the mobility and freedom of youth today. But the question of what sort of morality ought to be taught to those young people with all of this freedom is not changed by the fact that they have such freedom. Indeed, the existence of the freedom would point to the greater, not lesser, need for our children to internalize sound moral values based on a relationship to Jesus Christ at an earlier age, not to abandon values because parents cannot control their behavior as easily.

The presentation sounds suspiciously like the voice of the exasperated parent seeking justification for his or her failure to raise the children in the nurture and admonition of the Lord. What might be the compromised moral and spiritual values of the parents is pictured as the inevitible effect of social and technological evolution. We have bought the notion of the pampered style of life that adulthood means getting your way, or being able to do whatever you want. In fact adulthood means being mature enough in both knowledge and commitment so that you can be trusted to do the right thing even when no one is looking.

(6) Many in contemporary culture begin and establish a career at a later age than formerly. Marriage also tends to occur later. These two developments combined with convenient methods of birth control, the earlier onset of puberty and the absence of chaperonage, significantly lengthens the period when sexuality will be expressed outside of marriage.

The juggernaut of inevitability continues to build, with the assumption built-in that sexual expression is an obvious "necessity" and that denial of the "right" to this expression would be a violation of human nature. These factors are said to lengthen the period when sexuality *will be* expressed outside of marriage. The impression is that we could hardly expect our young adults to do otherwise -- which is gratuitous nonsense. We are continually presented with a *fait accompli* tied to the illogical conclusion that this *"fait"* is therefore necessarily a good and desireable thing.

(7) The gradual, but perceptible changes in attitude regarding what constitutes a 'complete' human being: the human body and sex are no longer considered something to be ashamed of, and these physical realities as well as intellect and spirituality constitute essential elements in the development of a complete human being.

It is implied that traditional Biblical morality is the product of the dualism that crept into Christian thinking, partly from Greek and other pagan influences, and that a healthy Hebraic outlook would abandon such moral restrictions. There simply is no direct connection between a healthy moral code and shame for one's body. A Biblically founded moral code is all about what one does with God's *good* creation, including one's body. The

23

goodness of the creation empowers the moral code and gives it deeper meaning rather than undermines it.

(8) The decline of exclusive male economic hegemony, which has resulted in a realignment of the male/female relationships in society.

"Patriarchy" and "exclusive male economic hegemony" are key issues. Pressure toward rejection of Biblical authority often comes from the camp which is having great trouble with the alleged patriarchy of Scripture. It is a view which has difficulty with *any* authority at all, i.e. not surprisingly, with the masculine side of the spectrum of life.

The realignment of male/female relationships in secular society is apparently being taken as a model for what they should be happening in the Biblical community. One might question the wisdom of the realignment, if by that is meant the pursuit by women of the masculine role at the very time when that role in western civilization is collapsing right out from under the males.[12] That there has been a realignment is unquestionable, but that the realignment is either rational or in accord with the will of God is hardly so certain.

(9) The existence of a better educated society, which does not depend upon authorities to determine 'what is right' on issues such as nuclear war or power plants, abortion, birth control, poverty, environment, etc.

(10) The intensifying clash between the claims of traditional authority as demanded by the family, church and society and the aims of twentieth century men and woman to seek their own fulfillment in ways that were not necessarily acceptable in the past. This is, of course, an ancient tension; it gains its particular contemporary character in American soci-

---

12 Several authors have written on this matter of the failure of nerve of the males in our culture, both secular and religious. Leanne Payne writes from a Christian point of view in CRISIS IN MASCULINITY, Crossway Books 1985, Westchester, Ill.

My article, "Sexuality, Gender, and Renewal" deals with these issues in the context of the masculine role in spiritual renewal. See endnote on Emmaus Ministries.

From a secular point of view, see Terry Burrows, "A Call to Men Therapists -- About Men", THERAPY NOW MAGAZINE, Summer 1984, p. 47 ff. PO Box 683, Station P, Toronto, Ontario, Canada M5S 2Y4. Also see Keith Thompson's article, "Robert Bly - What Men Really Want", NEW AGE, May 1982, p. 31 ff.

ety from the dissolution of the degree of ethical consensus as the society has become increasingly pluralistic.

The two final points both reflect two of the major issues, the rejection of authority in our culture and the acceptance of a pluralistic way of life. There can be a healthy side to both of these issues, but equally these two aspects of our culture can represent a rejection of the Biblical worldview at its very foundations.

The ten points are presented so as to make it appear that the onward march of progress makes the rejection of traditional moral standards inevitable, and that to clash with the "new" morality is to clash with human progress. Let us look more deeply at some of the presuppositions of this report which have in fact determined the outcome of its conclusions, perhaps far more than the cultural issues on which it claims to base itself.

B. Kingdom or Realm? The Loss of Personal Focus

Section I-B of the report is entitled, "The Centrality of Christ and the Realm of God". The report says,

> The central fact about Jesus's life and teaching is that he manifested in his relationships, acts, and words, the immanent and future Kingdom of God, which will be referred to as the Realm of God.

I was giving a lecture recently (spring 1987) at an Episcopal seminary in the course of which I was challenged concerning my masculine references to God. When I asked what kind of language would be acceptable, the student replied that she would rather talk of the "realm" of God rather than the "kingdom" of God on the grounds that "realm" did not have quite the same hierarchical and patriarchal thrust as "kingdom".

Back in the 1960's we experienced the phenomena of the "death of God." But a careful examination shows that only a very specific God died, and that another took its place. The God that died was the God "out there", the God of the heavens. On the other hand, the God that remained was the God of the "depths", and the God "within". Put in mythological and psychological terms, it was Father God who died and Mother God who survived. The death of God was really the death of Father, the God who stands independently of the cosmos in favor of God who is identified with the cosmos. The God who remained, or toward which we were steadily drifting, was none other than an updated version of the "Great Mother" of pagan mythology, the self-contained, self-sufficient cosmos, divine and eternal in her own nature, the divinity of the Perennial philosophy, signified in Scripture by the Tree of the Knowledge of Good and Evil, and her consort the serpent, the now fallen father image.

The truth is that Father God did not really die in this scenario, He was simply demoted to the image of the "kept man" of the Great Mother, who would occasionally strut his stuff to create the illusion of an authentic masculinity. The last thing the Serpent would want would be the revelation of a healthy and creative and complementary masculine-feminine relation in God in which image we could also be made.

The notion that God is deeply and intimately identified with His creation has always been a theme central to mainstream Christianity. The pendulum has often swung between immanence and tranuscendence in one direction or the other depending on the age and circumstances, but never has the Church lost sight of that truth as a basic part of Biblical and apostolic teaching. To treat the matter as though it were a recent discovery of liberal theology is to misread the facts of Christian history.

On the other hand, when we lose sight of the separateness of God from the cosmos, that He is indeed the personal and independent Creator of all else, then the notion of the immanence of God collapses into pantheism and monism. It becomes increasingly impossible to distinguish between God and the cosmos, the first and basic tenant of paganism. Once that happens, all of the other characteristics of the Perennial view listed above in Part I, and many others, follow closely behind. The *essential* gift of understanding from the Hebrew Scriptures to us is the notion that God is sole and sovereign creator of all else that is. God is I AM, He who stands alone, independently of and sovereign over all else. Such a notion was hardly broached in any other culture, and never carried out with consistency, such that a people of God could form under it. The clear distinction between God and His cosmos is the continental divide between Biblical and secular/pagan.

God, on the Biblical view, is intimately concerned with His creation. But He is so not by being one and the same with the cosmos, but by inhabiting it. God is creating a Temple fit to be His dwelling. He is creating a family in whose hearts He will dwell.

The use of the term 'realm' is not in itself pernicious. After all, God does have a realm. But when it is used deliberately to contrast with 'kingdom', then something is afoot. 'Realm' says something different from 'kingdom', which is precisely why it is chosen. It is that *difference* that we need to investigate.

'Kingdom', as the seminary student noted, has a masculine ring to it. It implies a king with attendant submission of subjects. It implies hierarchy and obedience. The apparently contrary value being sought by those who wish to use such language is "inclusiveness". "Kingship" is identified with exclusiveness whereas "realm" has to do with space and spaciousness and inclusiveness, feminine characteristics by contrast. It is certainly true that the feminine archtypal image has the qualities of inclusiveness, receptivity, and integration, whereas the masculine side has by definition the qualities of analysis, distinction, and at least potential exclusion.

In short, the term 'realm' is chosen with the specific aim in mind of excluding (!) the masculine side. The masculine side is seen as the enemy of the inclusiveness of the feminine side of God. In at least this sense, the report of the Diocese of Newark is a direct descendent of the death of God theology of the '60's and has back-slidden into pagan theology. The theme of inclusiveness occurs regularly throughout the report, whereas the theme of exclusiveness does not occur (except by implication to apply to those of a traditional Biblical view of sexual morality).

One of the most distressing characteristics of the Perennial view is its total and inherent inability to resolve the "battle of the sexes". The conflict between the masculine and feminine sides of life is unavoidable in a view of life centered on the "Great Mother" image of the self-sufficient cosmos.[13]   That is not to cast aspersions on the feminine image, but rather to point to the fact that the pagan/secular view is saddled with built-in paradoxes and contradictions. Neither the masculine nor the feminine images stand up very well. In the Biblical view, the masculine and feminine sides of life are in perfect union. As mentioned above, the Bible begins and ends in a marriage. We would normally take that marriage to be that of Adam and Eve in the Garden. But there is another and eternal marriage revealed prior to that, the marriage of the masculine and feminine in God, in the sacramental image of which Adam and Eve were to be made, male and female.

The Bible is not, in the sense that some have claimed, a "patriarchal" book. It is a book about the complementary union of masculine and feminine in the only pattern by which they can be successfully united, the pattern reflected throughout the Scriptures. That is not to say that the matter does not occasionally get out of balance in the Biblical community. Indeed it does. But the balance, as with any pendulum, swings in both directions. The problem is not that there is a differrence between the masculine and feminine which only a unisex program can eliminate, but rather than in our differences we become trapped in a power struggle, each side using its particular gifts to manipulate and to subject the other to its will. The Biblical doctrines of salvation and grace and sanctification are the solution to the battle of the sexes. But that is another story.[14]

The "realm" of God is a kingdom. There is no way around that. God is the "Boss". There is an hierarchy with God at the top. And furthermore, there is and will always be hierarchies in the human situation. To talk of a "realm" without a king is to play with words to give ourselves the impression of having said something Biblical when in fact we have taken the substance and meaning right out of the notion. The problem is not hier-

---

13 For further information on these issues, see my tapes A-1.1, A-1.2, and A-2. My book, YAHWEH AND THE GREAT MOTHER, which deals in depth with such issues, will be available in the summer of 1988 (see endnote on Emmaus Ministries).

14 See my tapes, C-1 through C-5 on Jesus and New Testament doctrine, also the "D" series on sexuality, for clarification on what Jesus has to do with our understanding of and participation in sex roles. See endnote on Emmaus Ministries for further information.

archies, but rather the power struggle into which
we are catapulted when we are not living by grace
and when hierarchy therefore becomes just another
tool in the power struggle.

C. The Problem of Authority

   As indicated above, the business of "inclusiveness" or of "inclusive language" revolves largely
around the problem of authority. It would appear
from the report that what is meant to be included
is the marginalized people of our culture and those
who in their rightful pursuit of life had been
denied access to the ministry of the Church. The
three groups concerning whom the report is made
(the young adults involved in extra-marital sexual
relationships, the elderly doing the same, and homosexual relationships) are the cases in point.

   Strikingly, the main burden of the report is
not seriously to address the rightness or wrongness
of the specific activities of any of these groups.
It is assumed that the activities in question are
in fact good and that it is the Church that needs
repentance, not the groups in question. Up is
called down, right is called left, evil is called
good, and we nod seriously and mutter, "How profound. How profound. Why didn't we see that before?" The disaster brazenly stares us in the face
and we are transfixed into passivity and "inclusiveness".

   The case presented rests almost entirely on
the alleged social conditions and pressures of our
culture, on the nature of the Church as an "inclusive" community, and tacitly on what is in fact a
materialist version of our sexual nature. At no
point is it asked, "Does God really want this?"
with any sort of evidence presented to back up the
claims. The matter is treated as essentially a
sociological or psychological or a biological urge
issue, with hardly a hint that God might have an
opinion about the matter. The *will* of God has been
effectively factored out of the equation.

      Today, the Church is no longer the single arbiter
   in these matters.... (p. 2) The existence of a better educated society, which does not depend upon
   authorities to determine 'what is right'.... (p. 3)

29

Not only is the Church no longer the single arbiter, neither is God. And the reason is clear, we are better educated so that we can discover the truth about life for ourselves and do not need to ask God or the Church anymore. In abstract theory one can approach God with or without the Church so that in abstract theory eliminating the Church as an arbiter might not be thought to be disasterous. But in fact, we are all constantly in need of a body of Christians who can give us feedback, advice, direction, and correction. To eliminate the visible Church and its authority is effectively to erode our ability to hear God accurately in large areas of our live. The fallen aspect of any of us does not take easily to being under authority, not even, nay especially, God's authority, and so any move the effect of which is to curtail God's authority in our lives is suspect.

But surely the writers of the report are Christian people who are seeking the will of God, are they not? And do they not say that Christ is the center of this "realm of God"? One cannot build windows into men's hearts to assess their innermost motives. The writers of the report may be honest seekers after the truth. But one must nevertheless judge the effects and meanings of words and deeds on their own merits. The thoughts expressed, not only in this report but in a great deal of theology today, betray a clear avoidance of the notion of the will of God and of our dependency on Him, precisely what one would expect from a theology which had suffered the "death of God" as outlined above.

The pattern is that of the forbidden tree..."For God knows that when you eat of it your eyes will be opened, and you will be like God, knowing good and evil." The forbidden tree is the tree of universal knowledge, the tree of omniscience, the kind of knowledge that would make one like God, the tree of independence and self-sufficiency. If you know it all, you do not need God. But God is not giving us knowledge so that we can learn our lessons and then run off to accomplish our own agenda with that knowledge. He gives us knowledge so that we might better cooperate with *His* plan for the cosmos and for our personal lives. The contrast between the person submitted to God and the person who tries to be the master of his soul and the captain of his fate is not that the secular humanist uses his intellect whereas the person submitted to God does not. Rather the difference is simply the *use* to which our minds are put. We will use our minds *either* to obey and cooperate with God and live, *or* to rebel and turn away and die. We delude ourselves to think either that we can use our minds to function in a secular way self-sufficiently, or that "those religious folk" do not use their minds. With God or without, we will use our minds. It is only a matter of whether well or poorly. Being religious does not imply being a muddleheaded thinker. If there is a correlation between religion and clear thinking, it may be quite the other way around.[15]

The connection, for example, between technology and science on one hand and the traditional Biblical morality on the other is not that technology will lead to the abandonment of Biblical morality because we have outgrown it, but rather that fallen man will always attempt to twist God's gifts to his own ends. We *want* to believe that our technology will make us self-sufficient and independent and autonomous. But not in one single instance can it be shown that that is in fact what is happening. We become *relatively* more independent, children do grow up and leave home. But the basic dependencies for meaning and existence remain. Not once has technology ever by itself made life objectively more meaningful. Convenient, yes, easier, yes. Objectively meaningful, no. We begin to treat as truth and life what in plain demonstrable fact is nonsense. It takes more than technology and expertise to give meaning to life. It takes a significant and obedient relationship with God. The serpent lied.

It is true that our better educated laity can answer certain questions without benefit of clergy. Thanks be to God. But the essential question that we must be asking is the one avoided by the report, namely, "Does God have a will in this matter?" Our minds are to help us discern and understand the will of God, not substitute for it. That is the glory of the human mind, that it can sufficiently for human requirements, grasp the nature and will of God. The primary function of our intellects and

---

15 Allan Bloom, in THE CLOSING OF THE AMERICAN MIND, does not try to prove a case for Christianity or religion. But nearly all of his arguments are in fact powerful ammunition to support the contention, which I would hold, that only with the Biblical God are we able to sustain a grasp on objective truth, and that once we lose that Biblical foundation our sense of objectivity and therefore the functioning of our reasoning begins to erode.

intuitive powers is not to become so smart as to be independent of God, an illusory goal, but rather to become wiser in our service to Him and more dedicated in our worship of Him, that is, more fully, not less, under His authority. "Unless you become as little children...."

Our educational programs, no matter how successful, can in principle never free us from the need for authority. Being under authority is not a matter of education or the lack of it. One cannot circumvent the need for authority by intelligence. The primary question of value and morality and direction in life is not a question that intelligence can answer by itself, for all of those items depend for their very meaning on our purpose for existence. And the only way you can find out why something exists is to ask the person responsible for its existence.[16] To find out why we exist, to find out the meaning of life, we must ask God. We can guess at it on our own, but we cannot independently know it. And if the meaning and goal of life turns out to be the Kingdom of God, and even if we should guess that correctly, clearly it is still idle to talk of in practical fact having a Kingdom of God without God as the King.

On a more practical and immediate level, we are all constantly depending on experts and authorities to make decisions for us. It is idle likewise to talk as though our educational systems have freed us from authorities. In fact, our education and technology and science have so complicated life that we are all depending increasingly, not less, on a host of authorities, medical, political, social, etc., whom we hope will help us make some reasonable sense of our circumstances. At every election time, every time we consult a doctor, we appoint people other than ourselves to make far reaching decisions for our lives. Whether we like the idea or not, we put a heavy burden on them to *know what is right for us*. Most of us are not equipped to make many of those decisions. We have neither the time nor the inclination nor the expertise to do so.

---

16 See my article, "Defining 'Oughtness' and 'Love'", JOURNAL OF RELIGION, July, 1959, p. 170 ff. The article gives the case to show that all objective morality depends on there being a purpose for existence, and hence a Purposer for existence. Reprints available from Emmaus Ministries (see endnote).

If that is true in politics or in medicine, it is equally true in religion. Not many people are independently equipped to make profound theological judgements for themselves, let alone for a community of people. Most people do not have the time or the inclination or the expertise, just as in politics. We may all fancy ourselves as armchair experts able to solve the issues of the world, but when it comes to actually making responsible decisions that effect our lives and the lives of thousands of people, few would want to bear the burden. It is not true, theoretically or practically, to suppose that the Church no longer has the task of spiritual leadership for society on the grounds that we are all able now to make such decisions for ourselves. The confusion and despair caused among the laity, not to mention the empty pews, when clergy give contradictory signals is living proof of this.

If it were true that we had become so gifted, one would expect the fruit of consistent decisions spontaneously in agreement among the population. What we in fact see is increasing chaos on all fronts, economic, political, moral, spiritual, and cultural, which we dignify with the title, "Pluralism". Instead of a spontaneous unity and harmony, we see unparalleled conflict and degradation of human life. The evidence of contemporary history indicates not that we have come of age, but that we have arrived at an unprecedented arrogance and self-delusion. Isaiah says of the idolator, "He feeds on ashes; a deluded mind has led him astray, and he cannot deliver himself or say, 'Is there not a lie in my right hand?'" (44:20)

The practical question we face is not one between "authority" versus "individual decision", but rather over *which* group, *which* community, *which* living tradition is the most trustworthy to point us on to God and to make certain decisions for us? We do not lose our individuality by being under authority. On the contrary, that is where we gain and exercise it. We acquire authority by being under it. We become made in the image of that authority and we live in the world bearing that authority, ultimately the Author-ity of God Himself, the Author.

D. Pluralism, Inclusiveness, and Relative Truth

Inclusiveness is the value in the Newark report held high like a banner. As with the term 'realm' there is nothing inherently pernicious about wanting to be inclusive. Jesus did indeed say, "Come unto Me, all ye that travail and are heavy laden, and I will refresh you," and many other similar things. And it is a basic Biblical testimony that God loves the whole of His creation and is inviting each of us into His kingdom. None of us will be excluded by *His* design. But it is also a basic Biblical principle that it is into *His Kingdom* that we are all being invited. He is not inviting us to come in and rearrange His furniture for Him. There are specific requirements for entry, the first of which being that we receive it as a gift, and the second of which being that we check our sins at the door. If we should be of a mind that we prefer our sins to His kingdom, then we shall have our sins but not His Kingdom. Sin is anything that works against the family life of those gathered under God as our Father.

Jesus is as inclusive as anyone can possibly be and still maintain the integrity of that Family. But He makes it quite clear that He is not kidding about sin. "Do not think that I have come to bring peace on earth; I have not come to bring peace, but a sword. For I have come to set a man against his father, and a daughter against her mother...." (Mt. 10:34) Jesus did not come just to pick fights. The sword is the Sword of the Spirit, the word of truth, "piercing to the division of soul and spirit, of joints and marrow, and discerning the thoughts and intention of the heart." (Heb. 4:12) The truth does indeed exclude all that is not of itself. Falsehood and lies and deceit, rebellion and disobedience cannot enter the Kingdom.

Episcopalians pray in The Great Litany for God to deliver us "from all inordinate and sinful affections; and from all the deceits of the world, the flesh, and the devil."[17] He can deliver us from them only by excluding them. The Perennial philosophy will not have any place in the Kingdom, and all within us that is of that way contrary to God's way will have to die before we can enter. I refer the reader to THE GREAT DIVORCE by C. S.

---

17 Episcopal BOOK OF COMMON PRAYER, p. 149. Seabury Press, New York, 1979.

Lewis, one of the most profound books ever written on the matter of judgement and hell, inclusion and exclusion.

We have all suffered under a legalistic exclusivism and under a twisted notion of God that perverted our perception of the God and Father of Jesus. If the "inclusive" program of the report were a corrective for that perversion, Christians could rejoice. But the program is not wanting merely to correct imbalance, it is wanting totally to deny the other half of the balance. Inclusiveness comes to mean nothing if there is not also a righteous exclusiveness. Our "yes" can mean nothing if we are not capable of saying "no". That is why we have to go through the "terrible two's", saying "no" to everything, and through the adolescent rebellion, to establish our ability to define our own sense of direction. If the Kingdom of God cannot say "no", it loses its identity. If the Kingdom is to be that "coincidence of opposites", the moral mish-mash which is typical of pagan notions of ultimate reality, trying to balance good and evil within itself, then it will not be worth the effort to get there. The "Kingdom" will prove to be simply that state of ambiguity and confusion in which the fallen world already lives.

> Our understanding of the Church is one of inclusiveness. As we struggle to understand what the Church is called to in our time, one of our goals is inclusion in the Christian body of persons who have thoughtfully chosen lifestyles different from that of the mainstream. (p. 12-13)

Taken out of context, this appears to be a perfectly acceptable sort of statement that a compassionate Christian might make. It is unquestionably God's plan and desire to include every last person in His Kingdom. But in the context, the cash value of "thoughtfully chosen" above is not clearly spelled out. Thoughtfulness in and of itself is a virtue, but hardly sufficient by itself to make a case. Hitler was very thoughtful about his "final solution", as have been many other evil-minded people. We ask the further question, Upon what basis is the thinking founded? The law and any kind of structure that might conflict with autonomous decision making is constantly put in a negative light throughout the report. God, the

Kingdom, and human nature are all treated as though they were more or less structureless entities, freely to be molded by our personal desires.

Jesus said on one occasion when His disciples had plucked grain in the field on the Sabbath, "The sabbath was made for man, not man for the sabbath; so the Son of man is lord even of the sabbath." (Mk. 2:27) God had not sat down at the beginning of creation and invented a set of admirable laws, and then thought to Himself, "Well. Now I need some people to obey and lift up and honor these laws!" Rather He created people, and then thought to Himself, "These people will need some laws to keep them pointed in the right direction should they wander off the lighted path." The laws are for *our benefit.* God does not need directions, for He, and He alone, already understands everything. We need laws for those situation when we are not living in grace, not intuitively in touch with reality, and cannot for ourselves see what God wants us to do. The law is God's safety net to catch us when we fall out of grace, as well as His warning sign to us as to the kinds of behavior we have to check at the Pearly Gates.

> The relativizing impact of the Realm of God enables us to see more clearly what Biblical and historical research discloses: that beliefs and practices surrounding marriage and sexuality have varied according to time, culture and necessity. (p. 5)

The "realm of God" as pictured by the report does indeed have a relativizing impact. But the Kingdom of God pictured in the Old and New Testaments does no such thing. Of course beliefs and practices have varied, partly because most cultures had their beginnings devoid of any contact with the Gospel. But that is not even evidence, let alone proof, for the notion that therefore the Biblical community can have no clear and definite understanding of God's intention for us. J. I. Packer writes in THE EVANGELICAL CATHOLIC:

> The Bultmannite hermeneutic, which treats New Testament narrative and theology as so much culture-determined mythology, celebrating and evoking the ineffable impact of God upon us while telling us nothing of a divine-human redeemer at all, has bred a worldwide crop of Christian reconstructionists, all starting from a non-incarnational view of Jesus, all working with a unitarian idea of God seasoned with more or less of process-theology, all claiming that

36

modern secular knowledge makes their type of view
the only one possible, and all vigorously offsetting
themselves from the categories and content of traditional belief.[18]

Packer is referring to the relativizing impact,
not of science or anthropology, still less of the
true realm of God, but rather of the philosophical
attitude of these "reconstructionists". The God of
the reconstructionists is, as Packer indicates,
"ineffable", a term commonly used in the Perennial
view of God, indicating that God is not describable
in propositional terms. That is a view which makes
no sense in any event, but it certainly has no
place in the Bible where God is continually revealing Himself in quite clearly propositional language. He speaks a "word" to us, and expects us to
understand it clearly enough so that we can rationally respond to it. An ineffable God cannot do
that.

A consequence of the Perennial loss of a sense
of objectivity is the very uneasy feeling that God
is a kind of unknowable, mysterious, and indeterminate something-I-know-not-what. If that is indeed
the truth about God, then He is incapable of being
made relevant to our present life. If there are no
objective truths we can know about God, then we had
best leave the whole matter alone. Religion then
really is for all we can know a projection of our
father-(or mother-)figures upon the universe, as
per Freud.

The Biblical view of God's relation to the world
is that the world is meant to *reveal* Him, to shine
with His glory in ways that would draw praise and
awe and wonder from us -- and understanding of the
mind. There are certainly things about God that
are difficult, perhaps impossible, to put into
words. But that does not mean that there are *no*
truths about God that we cannot reliably put into
words. There are, and we can. Bultmann and the
reconstructionists have fallen prey to a God which
is at home in the self-contained world of the
Perennial philosophy, not in the Christian faith.

It is pointed out (p. 5) that marriage was not
given sacramental status in the Church until 1439,
implying that the sacredness of marriage is only an
historically relative matter which can be reversed
when the circumstances require. The possibility

---

18 J. I. Packer, "How Do We Comprehend?", THE EVANGELICAL CATHOLIC, April 1987, p. 8.

that this decision was in response to the Holy
Spirit guiding the Church to invest physical and
historical realities with eternal significance is
not considered. But it is claimed, on the other
hand, that the reversal of this is indeed of the
Holy Spirit:

> The challenge to the Church to respond creatively to
> changing patterns of sexuality and family life in
> America must be seen as an instance of the Holy
> Spirit leading us... (p. 4)

The sacramental view of the Bible does not inform us that God is an image-less-something-or-oth-
er devoid of content to be grasped by human mind,
intuition, or imagination. The two central doctrines of Christendom, the doctrine of creation and
the doctrine of the Incarnation, both directly
imply that God is an imaginable God. Firstly, we
are told that we are made in His image, so that
just to know a human being is to have some access
to knowledge about God (see also Mt. 25:31 ff.).
And secondly, the effect of the Incarnation is to
make that God in whose image we are made all the
more imaginable: "He who has seen me has seen the
Father." (John 14:9) We can *know* in the most deep
and profound way this Creator who stands independently of His cosmos. And every part of our knowing apparatus will be drawn in to receive this
Self-disclosure of God.

Institutions like marriage can certainly be made
into idols. Biblical history has been littered
with gifts from God that have become blocks to God
rather than windows to God. And like many things
in the religious life, this needs correcting. The
Hebrews did it with the law and the Temple; Christians have done it and are doing it with the institutional Church, with the Bible, and with the
sacraments. But that fact does not invalidate the
significance of God's creation as a sacrament of
Himself, that precise and determinate truths about
God and His plan for us can be and are being revealed through the events and objects of time and
space and history, and that these truths are to be
believed and followed. This basic Biblical principle is denied by the report ironically in the
name of the Incarnation:

The dynamic process of God's incarnational truth has brought us to a time in history when the critical consciousness made possible by modern forms of knowledge - including Biblical scholarship - enables us to see the Realm of God as a present reality relativizing all human knowledge and social arrangements. (p. 9)

This Perennial process of relativizing is *not* the same as the Biblical process of bringing our idolatry of the world under subjection to the will of God. In fact the two work in exactly opposite directions, for the relativizing process of which the report so glowingly speaks makes the will of God both unintelligible and irrelevant. The Perennial relativizing process soon makes it impossible to distinguish between the will of God and whatever cultural trend is happening down the road, leading to the most profound and destructive and therefore evil of idolatries.

As Bloom indicates in THE CLOSING OF THE AMERICAN MIND, Nazis in Germany were so idolatrously identified with the sweep of their history and culture that they could no longer distinguish between themselves and the will of God. All truth was relative indeed. It was not mentioned that what it was relative to was *their* perception of life and value, but certainly not to any Source of life and value above and beyond themselves. The same occurred to Communist intellectuals in Hungary and Poland during the 1950's, who became aware that they were losing their ability to distinguish between truth and falsehood, they had lied and twisted the truth to fit the party line so long.[19] Happily, many of them rebelled and dedicated themselves to presenting the truth as they perceived it, whether the Party liked it or not.

King David's submission to Nathan the prophet (II Sam. 11-12) over the matter of Uriah and Bathsheba signaled a monumental change in the Hebrew attitude toward kingship from that of the surrounding pagans. David clearly saw himself accountable to Someone higher than himself -- whereas the pagan kings typically considered themselves above the law, especially with respect to those of lower station in life.

---

19 Michael Polanyi referred to this matter in some of his lectures at Oxford University, 1962-3. See, MEANING, by Michael Polanyi and Harry Prosch, Chicago University Press, Chicago, 1975, p. 24.

The relativizing which the Spirit of God accomplishes is to highlight the world as relative, to be sure -- *but as relative to God and to the will of God*. (It makes no logical sense to call something "relative" without specifying that *to* which it is relative.) But the effect of the Biblical kind of relativizing is as an act of grace to give to the world, which is contingent and dependent and therefore without eternal and objective meaning, that very meaning and glory and life which are eternal with increasing clarity and precision, not ambiguity lost in confusion.

The pluralism of which the report speaks approvingly and as an inevitability, is a reflection not of a practical difficulty of the moment in establishing the truth of a matter. It is a far more profound contemporary disbelief in there being any objective truth at all. That is the ground of the so-called "inclusiveness" of the report and of much contemporary theology. Where there is no objective ground for difference, there is also no ground for exclusion. Where there is no objective truth by which our personal opinions might be tested, then there is no good reason for excluding another man's version of the truth. We get into the Dodo bird's Caucus Race where everybody wins and everybody gets a prize.

> Thus, truth in the Judeo-Christian tradition is a dynamic process to be discerned and formulated rather than a static structure to be received. (p. 3)

This is the "process theology" to which J. I. Packer pointed in the quote above. Truth has no ultimate anchor point, no fixed foundation. Or, the foundation is that ineffable I-know-not-what, hidden mysteriously behind all phenomena, never revealing itself, but always teasing us into believing it is going to say something intelligent with "manifestations" or "avatars" (to use the Hindu word). Since the basic reality is totally indeterminate, absolutely anything, no matter how contradictory, will fit. Which of course makes it also absolutely useless to tell us anything.

Edmond Browning, Presiding Bishop, offered at the September 1987 meeting of the House of Bishops as his eighth mission imperative:

...."last but by no means least"--is the continuing commitment to the search for unity "of the Church and of all God's people." He called the Church to move beyond ecumenical dialogue to "a realistic world view of interfaith dialogue with Islam, Judaism, Hinduism, and the other world religions. I want the Episcopal Church to live up to its global responsibilities."[20]

Without putting words in the bishop's mouth, one wonders whether "realistic world view of interfaith dialogue" means giving up claims that there are unique elements to the Gospel of Jesus Christ which cannot be bartered away or that the historic character of Jesus, the Son of God, makes the Christ event pivotal in human history. The global responsibilities of the Episcopal Church, if that is so, do not include the conversion of Muslims, Jews, and Hindus, or anybody else, to Jesus as Lord and Savior. The Great Commission has been exchanged for a round table sharing of viewpoints in which objective truth has disappeared, a kind of metaphysical wife-swapping, the contemporary version of Israel going a-whoring after false gods.

This relativizing reaches a climax in section V-C:

> Rather than arguing about these issues we need first to listen to the experience of those who are most directly involved.
>
> We need as much as is possible to bracket our judgements and listen to persons as they are.

Fair enough. But then...

> So the Church's response includes permitting itself to be ministered to by the homosexual community.
>
> Such words as ministry and hospitality, however, still suggest a relationship of inequality, we and they. As such they perpetuate the image of the Church as separate from the homosexual community. (p. 13-14)

We are encouraged to believe that the Church really has nothing to say to homosexuals about their lifestyle, and that for the Church to think it does is arrogant and closed minded. There is no possibility of judgement upon any lifestyle excepting from within the terms and conditions of itself.

---

20 *The Episcopalian*, November 1987, p. 14. See above, Part I, Section A, "Clearing Our Vision", for comments on his seventh point.

That is, there is no possibility of judgement on any lifestyle. Not even God can break in. (Let it be noted that accurately describing behavior is not the kind of judgement forbidden by Jesus in Matthew 7:1. We are forbidden to condemn persons, not behavior, as Jesus indicates by His own activity.)

It is indeed encumbant upon each of us to listen with compassion and to get the facts, as the report urges. But "bracketing our judgements" and an attitude of listening does not legitimately mean letting go of our moral standards to let the world dictate to the Christian community what its standards must be. The Church is indeed inclusive, everyone is invited in. But no one is invited into the house of God to come in and reorder the furniture to their own liking. The community itself discerns as nearly as it can where God wants the furniture, and that is where it stays. If it turns out that God is speaking a word to the Church through those being ministered to, with all honesty and charity, that will have to be discerned for the Church by the leadership and membership of the Church, not by those who come for ministry. The matter was put very succinctly by St. Benedict:

BENE DICTUM, BENEDICTE!

If any pilgrim monk come from distant parts, if with wish as a guest to dwell in the monastery, and will be content with the customs which he finds in the place, and do not perchance by his lavishness disturb the monastery, but is simply content with what he finds, he shall be received, for as long a time as he desires. If, indeed, he find fault with anything, or expose it, reasonably, and with the humility of charity, the Abbot shall discuss it prudently, lest perchance God had sent him for this very thing. But, if he have been found gossipy and contumacious in the time of his sojourn as guest, not only ought he not to be joined to the body of the monastery, but also it shall be said to him, honestly, that he must depart. If he does not go, let two stout monks, in the name of God, explain the matter to him.[21]

---

21 I copied this from either a wall plaque or brochure during a stay at the Mount Calvary Retreat House in Santa Barbara, California in September, 1967.

E.   Laws and Human Nature

The loss of a sense of objectivity encompasses
the nature of God, the nature of moral law, and
also the nature of humanity itself. The human race
is treated as though it had little or no determinate nature which needs to be respected in order
for that nature to run well. If one does not respect the nature of a car, and if in view of that
one does not follow the directions in the owner's
manual, one will shortly come to a bad end with his
car (as I once learned after putting off too long
adding oil to my crankcase).

Human nature likewise has a structure, and the
Maker has given us an Owner's Manual to let us know
how best to run it. The laws are designed to make
the machine run. This is not to glorify laws over
persons, but that does not alter the fact that
people had better obey the laws or the "machine"
will break down.

The report is not totally devoid of a sense of
human nature. But the human nature implied is
largely influenced and dominated by what is in fact
a materialist notion, with its roots in a Freudian-
Kinseyian-type belief that physical, genital sexuality is *the* basic human drive.[22]   In section
II-E, "Revised Understanding of the Person", we are
told that the traditional Biblical morality is the
product of Greek dualism and that contemporary culture, having overcome the dualistic rejection of
our physical and sexual side, has a more Hebraic
notion of ourselves.

> We do not *have* bodies, we *are* bodies, and the doc-
> trine of the Incarnation reminds us that God comes
> to us and we know God in the flesh. (p. 6)

> It is our conclusion that by suppressing our sexual-
> ity and by condemning all sex which occurs outside
> of traditional marriage, the Church has thereby ob-
> structed a vitally important means for persons to
> know and celebrate their relatedness to God. (p. 7)

---

22 See third chapter, *Science - the Poisoned Well*, for further comments on the Freudi-
an-Kinseyan background and reasons for doubting both the scientific and philosophical foundations of much of that source of current sexology.

The Hebraic insistence that our bodies are a
legitimate part of ourselves is a long distance
from the contemporary belief that we are essentially defined by our physical nature. We do not have
on the Biblical view the same relation to our bodies that we have to our souls. I do not lose my
identity if I lose an arm. Even a heart trans-
plant, though it may be an emotional trial, does
not produce a different *person.* Nor do I lose my
identity when I die and lose my physical body alto-
gether. I am promised a new body, but it is clearly not the same identical body as the previous one
moldering in the grave. We do indeed need a body,
but the body is the servant of the soul, not vice
versa. We are told to subject the body to the
spirit (I Cor. 9:27). The relation of the body to
the soul is to be the outward and visible sign of
the soul, a sacramental relation. The human nature
of the Newark report reflects a materialist Freudian background more akin to Canaanite paganism than
to Hebraic sacramentalism.

The clear implication of the report is that genital sexuality is a prerequisite for humanness. As
important as sexuality is in the Biblical culture,
it is not the basic foundation of our nature.
Physical sexuality is a sacrament of something more
basic, namely our masculine and feminine aspects.
The spiritual qualities of gender precede the biological qualities of sex. Biology is a sacrament
of the soul, not vice versa. Genital sexuality has
its rightful place, but it can never bear the burden our culture is placing upon it, a result of
which is to focus our attention on the world of the
closed, self-sufficient circle, neglecting the
weightier and deeper matters of the spirit of which
the world is to be a sacrament.

The deeper issue is gender, not sex. That is
the nature of our sacramental world. It is the
materialist view that will always divinize sex because it is an inheritor of the tremendous power
and dynamism of sex without any adequate explanation or experience of the source and meaning of it.
Human nature cannot be fullfilled merely by giving
free rein to our sexual appetites, curtailed only
by a necessarily vague concern for the "quality" of
the relationship. The quality of the relationship
will quickly enough erode because the objective
moral side of human nature has been ignored and
dismantled in our contemporary thinking. The rules
of chastity are given to us because there is an

objective need in each of us for consistent and permanent loyalty in sexual relationships. When that is violated, our inner being begins to collapse and sexuality ceases to be a sacrament of God and becomes instead a sacrament of the world, the flesh, and sooner or later, the devil.

What is the evidence of that? The daily news. It would be hard to find a single aspect of the contemporary experiment in sexual freedom of which it could be said, "Here is a success story." The report tells us,

> We cannot live without structure in our relationships; but these structures are subject to continual correction by the image of the Realm of God. (p. 8)

That is small comfort if the effect of the correction of the Realm of God is continually to tell us that these structures do not reflect anything that can be permanent and intelligible and meaningful. If one can never discover some concrete and particular meaning in the structure, something that one would be willing to stand on, even at the cost of his life, then the search for meaning is futile. It always disappears into that mysterious and ineffable I-know-not-what. The Ground of Being turns into Foggy Bottom.

> Our contemporary consciousness of racial, sexual, and economic domination and exploitation has raised our culture's consciousness about some of the oppressive, repressive and exploitative dimensions of marriage and family arrangements. This heightened sensitivity, combined with a cultural ethos that favors self-fulfillment over the dutiful but self-abnegating adherence to conventional marriage and family arrangements has caused many to deny that life-long monogamous, heterosexual marriage is the sole legitimate structure for the satisfaction of our human need for sexuality and intimacy. (p. 9)

It is the loss of the Fathering side of God which leads us directly into a pampered child style of life, which favors self-fulfillment over duty. The duty that God gives us is not, if carried out in a true relationship to Him, self-abnegating excepting in the sense that we are indeed called to "die to self". The pinch-faced Christian mournfully dragging his cross around is not fulfilling the Lord's command to pick up our crosses daily and follow Him. If we are really following Jesus, we can expect to go through dark valleys, perhaps depession, loneliness, and other difficult times, but the goal is still the Kingdom, the beauty and joy and power of which nothing in the world of the closed, self-sufficient cosmos can begin to approach.

There may happily be indeed a heightening of sensitivity among many contemporary people to the suffering of those around them. But that suffering will not be eased by ignoring the structure of human nature nor the laws meant to make that structure work well. As the saying goes, "When everything else fails............, read the directions."

What is heightened in so many cases is not a sensitivity to the suffering of other people, but rather an overweening self-centeredess. The obsessive concentration on self-fulfillment itself produces a dissatisfaction with legitimate duty or with anything else that contradicts the imperative wants of the pampered child within us.

> In the absence of set rules, great demands are thus placed on clergy and others who counsel... (p. 10)

That is something of an understatement. Counselors are asked either to find a way in a total void, where no way exists, or to simply go with the direction that the person has chosen for himself, even when one knows in his heart the wrongness of that direction before God.

> All relationships and arrangements are to be assessed in terms of their capacity to manifest marks of the Realm of God: healing, reconciliation, compassion, mutuality, concern for others both within and beyond one's immediate circle of intimacy. (p. 10)

The feminine characteristics are legitimately listed here, but there is a marked lack of the masculine side including righteousness, justice, definition, and a high and holy moral expectation, an unhappy combination that will surely feed and support the effort of the pampered child within us to claim his alleged "rights".

F. Judgementalism and the Judgement of God

We have said very little about the specific issues of the three sexual practices discussed in the
report: pre-marital sex, post-marital sex, and homosexual unions. Our purpose has been rather to
focus on the issues behind the issues, those principles which outline for us what is Biblical and
what is not. Unless we are secure and agreed on
those matters, our discussion about sexual morality
will not go very far. If persons wish to discuss
the issues on ground other than those outlined
above, which are the grounds traditionally called
"Biblical" for well over two millenia, then the
burden of proof is on such persons to show why
their new grounds still are deserving of the name
"Biblical" or "Christian".

Suffice it to say that the grounds given for
supporting such behavior, in this writer's experience, are heavily weighted in the self-centered
direction, even though they are freighted with
"concern" or "compassion" or "inclusiveness". The
"post-married" couple who are living together without benefit of marriage, for example, on the
grounds that they would lose economically were they
to marry (see page 12 of the report) is not a moral
issue so much as a convenience issue or a
life-style issue. The same sorts of arguments are
given for the abortion of an infant in the womb.
That I might be called to self-sacrifice, or that
we might do well to call each other to such
self-sacrifice, seems to be an unacceptable notion.

It is incredible to this writer that, given the
appalling tragedy of AIDS, the report can give such
a casual approval of the homosexual life-style and
mention nothing of that condition. It is indeed
difficult, in our present climate, to bring religion into the discussion without someone feeling
the hot breath of the Judgemental God down his
neck. A recent "Dear Abbey" letter was reacting
strongly to someone who had said that AIDS was a
punishment from God. The writer retorted that an 8
year old hemopheliac could not have broken any of
God's laws when he got aids through a blood trans-

fusion, nor could have any of the infants whose bodies are wracked with the incurable disease have offended God so badly that He would afflict them.

No one with an ounce of sense of the Gospel would maintain that such was the case. God does not set out to inflict us with any kind of vindictive punishment, "...for He does not willingly afflict or grieve the sons of men." (Lam. 3:33) One ventures onto very difficult ground in any explanation of the problem of pain, but some things are clear. We live in a cosmos and we share a human nature which makes us very vulnerable to the actions and reactions of one another. The world that God has created does have the possibility and indeed the reality of such events as infants with AIDS. Those facts must be reconciled with and contained within the greater fact of the love of an almighty Creator.

It is not judgemental to point out that the condition of AIDS appears to have been generated and continues to spread in conjunction with certain practices of a homosexual life style. It is not judgemental to point out that chastity is at present the *only* sure way of drastically curtailing the spread of that disease insofar as it is spread by sexual contact. And it is not judgemental, it is simply accurate, to point out that the very lack of the sense of the objectivity of morality and of human nature is playing a central part in the continuing spread of the disease, not only in sexually transmitted forms but also in drug needle transmitted forms, the only parallel for which in human history is the ravages of the medieval bubonic plagues.

Our obsession for our "rights", primarily our "right to feel good" (hence our burgeoning "condom morality"), is blinding us to the point of self-destruction. AIDS is only perhaps the most dramatic example of this inexcuseable behavior. For the first time in my life I understood the phrase, "bleeding heart liberal". If I had had AIDS, I would have screamed, "Damn your spineless compassion! Do something *effective*!" I do not have AIDS, and, with compassion and sincerity, I still say it.

A compassion that is not ultimately rooted in defending the honor of Jesus and in obedience to His word will turn out in the long run to be no compassion at all. Compassion that is spineless, compassion without backbone, compassion that has no toughness, is lethal. It is the kindness that kills. We are watching people die, in part because watchmen are abandoning their watchtowers and are calling no warning.

The Church will have no spiritually significant ministry to AIDS victims until the confusion and deception about the judgement of God has been resolved. The judgement of God is indeed one of the key issues to the whole range of sexual issues. St. John tells us what is the judgement of God:

> And this is the judgement, that the Light has come into the world, and men loved darkness rather than light, because their deeds were evil. (3:19)

Judgement happens whenever the Light comes into the world. We are judged by the very presence of God, like Amos's plumb line:

> Behold, I am setting a plumb line in the midst of my people Israel; I will never again pass by them; the high places of Isaac shall be made desolate, and the sanctuaries of Israel shall be laid waste.... (7:8)

When a plumb line is hung, the wall stands judged. When the Light shines into the world, the world stands judged. The judgement falls not only because the Light shines, but is confirmed and the sentence set because rather than repenting, we run for the darkness to hide our guilt. The judgement is simply: if you want to do it your way, you shall have it your way -- consequences and all. The darkness into which we run will not save us from our AIDS, there is no salvation there, no health, no wholeness, only the twisting and contorting of a world convulsed in the tragedy ultimately of its own choosing.

That is not to imply that the eight year old or the infant who has AIDS is either being punished by God or that that child has decided to run from God, even though that individual guilt might obtain in individual cases. But it is rather to say that the very context of our life support and nurturing and direction giving is disintegrating all around us. In the midst of that disintegration, there will be horrendous tragedy, the innocent will suffer, not by the will of God, but because our collective sin has so damaged the matrix of nurturing and growth which God planned for us. Mother Nature, Mother Land, and even Mother Church is sick unto death, and can hardly bring forth a healthy a child.

Laws are treated by many today as though they were threats from God, and since we now know that God is a loving God, we can assume that laws are no longer binding. Laws are oppressive and rigid and constricting.

But that is not a view of the law that one can construct from Scripture, either Old or New Testaments, neither Jesus nor Paul. The Perennial viewpoint is the source of such a view, not Scripture. Scripture views the law as a part of God's protection for mankind. All through the Old Testament and all through Jewish culture, the Law is an honor bestowed upon the chosen people. Jesus came to fulfill the law, not to abolish it (Mt. 5:17), and Paul thought of the ceremonial and sacrificial law as a tutor or custodian until grace should come (Gal. 3:24), and never once did he suggest that the moral law was less than to be followed, or that any one of the Ten Commandments had been suspended.

The law was given for our *protection*, not as a threat or in a negative sense as a judgement, just as an owner's manual is given for the protection of the owner of a new piece of equipment, not as a threat of what God will do if you do not put oil into your engine. When we abandon the law we step outside of God's protection. There is no other safe place for us to be than squarely in the will of God. To deny or compromise the will of God is in the final analysis, the final judgement, to sign our own death warrent.

We complain that the law is judging us, when it is we who are sitting in judgement on God, and then receive often enough in our own flesh the results of that judgement. It is a well known fact that thousands are dying, whether out of ignorance or rebellion, all over the world who would not be had they followed the direction God has given us.

A pastor recently noted that the Church itself has a lethal case of AIDS, Acute Immune Deficiency Syndrome. The Church has an acutely deficient immune system. Our immune system to fight off spiritual infection relies entirely on our hearing the word of God and on our obedience to it, and on our putting the full weight of our dependency on His

hand. The presence of God in our lives is our
immune system. When we close the circle of
self-sufficiency around us, when we try to live as
though the will of God were meaningless or irrelevant or out of date, then we become subject to the
diseases of a fallen world. And the wages paid by
sin is still death. We are receiving the very natural and inevitable consequences of choosing to
live out of touch with reality. It would appear
from medical reports that we have just begun to see
the terrible results of our perverseness with God.

Some have read the Newark report and responded,
upon finding that its conclusions are somewhat em-
barrassing, "They are not really *encouraging* such
behavior, they are only asking for an open discussion of the issues." The report, for all its fail-
ures, is written fairly clearly in the English language. It is difficult to see how it can be read
other than as encouraging the sexual permissiveness
discussed. The report hardly reads as though the
writers had not made up their minds on the issues.
As quoted above:

> *It is our conclusion* that by suppressing our sex-
> uality and by condemning all sex which occurs out-
> side of traditional marriage, the Church has thereby
> obstructed as vitally important means for persons to
> know and celebrate their relatedness to God. [empha-
> sis mine, p. 7]

Not only are firm conclusions drawn but there is no
serious discussion of alternative viewpoints other
than to insinuate that the genuinely Biblical alternatives are legalistic, rigid, and out of touch
with contemporary reality. There is no "minority
report".

The *effect* of the report certainly has been to
encourage discussion. But the clear intent of the
report goes beyond that to further the move into a
kind of sexual practice which for nearly 20 centuries of Christian history up until a decade ago
would have been called by all Christians licence
contrary to the will of God, that is to say, sin.

The report echoes and re-echoes the truth that
we are confronted with changing sexual patterns.
It also echoes the *non sequitur* that therefore we
had better get with the times if we are not to be
left behind as reality rolls on. Reality rolls on,
effectively divorced from the judgement of God.
The circle of the cosmos has closed. God, or at

least His will, has been declared null and void in favor of the drift of the times. Given the history of the world, our present world in particular, it strikes me as odd that people are so impressed with the drift of the times. No century in recorded history has shown such clear signs of drifting massively into narcissism, chaos, and self-destruction.

The only effective solution comes to us from the pages of ancient wisdom:

> If my people who are called by my name humble themselves, and pray and seek my face, and turn from their wicked ways, then I will hear from heaven, and will forgive their sin and heal their land. (2 Chron. 7:14)

That is a word to the Church, not to the unbelievers. It is a word to those who call themselves Christians to live lives of holiness and of joy and of a vibrant spirit, to be a sacrament of the life of God in the world. It is a word to the Bishop and Diocese of Newark and to every other diocese and parish in the land. We need to make some clear decisions, decisions which will cause lines to be drawn. But, they will be lines which will reveal the true nature of the King and of the Kingdom, and which will enable and encourage people of all circumstances to make a clear choice for God and for His Kingdom.

Epilogue:

Liberal and Conservative -- on the Three Legged Stool

The meaning of 'liberal' and of 'conservative' has changed with every age. This generation's liberalism becomes the next generation's conservatism. But there is a sense in which liberalism stands more for the adventure into new truth while conservatism stands for the preservation of old and established truth.

The connecting link is, of course, the "truth". Since truth cannot contradict itself, one would suppose that liberal and conservative would constantly find themselves running into agreement rather than the usual conflict. Our age has as much as any experienced this inner social and spiritual contradiction. We in the Anglican tradition are experiencing it in our confusion over gender issues such as the ordination of women to the priesthood and episcopate and gender inclusive language, over sexual morality, and even over the fundamental doctrinal teachings of the Anglican tradition, the place of Jesus, the meaning of the Trinity, the reality of the Resurrection. Much of this confusion is supposedly caused by the "modern mindset". The contemporary liberal approach tends to link itself with this modern mindset and with what might be called the secular attitude and the feeling that the human race can now manage its own affairs, having come of age.[23]

At one time, I considered myself a liberal. And in one important sense I still do. The liberals I admired when I was in college and seminary during the 1950's were persons who were dedicated to getting at the truth, no matter where the evidence led. I found myself unable to pit "truth testing" techniques (such as used in Biblical studies, to try to decide on historical evidence, for example, whether there were miracles or not) against my faith. If truth testing and faith could not stand together, neither one would stand very long.

I stood in the middle of my room one day at seminary, feeling depressed and discouraged over the issues. So I told the Lord that if there were miracles, that was fine, if there were not, that was fine, I just wanted to know which. If there were, they would have to stand on their own feet, and not be supported by an artificial claims to either Papal or Biblical infallibility or inerrancy. If God did not exist, I wanted to know that, if Jesus was in fact not the Son of God, I wanted to know that. I was willing to trust Him to sort that out in ways that really would make sense to me. I want to worship "I AM", not "I AM NOT" or "I CANNOT TELL YOU WHO I AM BECAUSE I AM NOT SURE

---

23 Allan Bloom's, THE CLOSING OF THE AMERICAN MIND, is an extraordinary critique of western, not just American, culture, a must for any Christian who wants to understand how to relate the Biblical framework to that of our times.

MYSELF". Moses ("Who am I that I should go to Pharoah....?") had the identity crisis at the Burning Bush, not God. (Ex. 3-4)

If all this seems to put the Christian faith at risk, indeed it does. It puts our faith at risk to the truth....which is to say that what we are really risking is not the truth at all, but only our prejudices, or (again to quote The Great Litany), "all false doctrine, heresy, and schism,... hardness of heart, and contempt of thy Word and commandment."[24] The fact that we feel so insecure about honest truth seeking at these deep levels shows how far we have indeed drifted from our Biblical roots.

My decision standing in the middle of my room was a leap of faith, not into the dark, but into the light. Somewhere along the way I discovered that the bottom foundation of Biblical faith is simply openness to the truth, a teachable spirit. Jesus said to His disciples, "If you continue in my word, you are truly my disciples, and you will know the truth, and the truth will make you free." (John 8:31-2) Apparently following Jesus is meant to be a course in living in the truth. Nowhere in Scripture is truth treated as an esoteric sort of thing. Truth is what you arrive at by honest inquiry, the sort of thing anyone might expect to be able to do, the teachable spirit. That does not rule out the need for revelation, it only says that even (nay especially) in our receiving of revelation we still need an open, inquiring, and clear thinking mind. Revelation does not mean our being a mindless blotter to God's rubber stamp. Spiritual maturity requires an intelligent dialogue between us and God.

The more I studied and lived my faith, the more I discovered that indeed in all of its essentials, including many "miracles", the Bible was quite capable of standing on its own feet. The essential message of creation and salvation more than stood the tests to which they were subjected. When the dust settles, they are left standing quite alone on the field of spiritual battle. There is no other way to make sense of the world and of life than the Biblical way. But one discovers that only by being open to the truth and by letting the tests of life be made, not by "protecting" the Bible or one's faith from those tests by delusions of infallibili-

---

24 Episcopal BOOK OF COMMON PRAYER, p. 149. Seabury Press, New York, 1979.

ty. God, who alone is infallible, is not protected by the likes of ourselves. The protection goes the other way.

The liberal gift to the Church, which must be honored if the Christian community is to move from its position of impotence and irrelevance to the world around us, is the gift of the pursuit of truth. That means that there will always be a kind of open-endedness to our lives, a risk. "Faith" must include at the root of its meaning, "openness to the truth, whatever it may be, at any cost to ourselves." We must be correctible by the truth. We must be dedicated to getting the truth and living it. The Gospel on any other grounds is at best immaturity and at worst a fraud. It is into that openness to the truth that God called Abraham, Moses, and the prophets, that Jesus called His disciples, and that God through the Holy Spirit is calling us today, trusting that in that open exchange with reality, God will indeed reveal Himself. How else would a God of sacramental history reveal Himself? And how else could the truth set us free?

But open-endedness does not mean lack of commitment, or an inability to make decisions or to commit oneself to a course of moral and spiritual action in obedience to God. It is rather that which frees us from narrow minded legalism and makes us correctible by God, the ultimate Reality who calls us into this journey of faith. It is hard, objective reality into which we are called, as C. S. Lewis portrays so well in THE GREAT DIVORCE, not merely into our own personal and therefore relative opinions.[25] Reality does not get out of the way for anybody.

The conservative gift is to call us to stand on that objective reality. The moment one, in the course of his liberal search for the truth, decides to make a stand on a given position, he becomes a conservative.

---

25 In this extraordinary bus trip from hell to heaven, the inhabitants of hell find the setting of heaven quite disconcerting, everything seems to hard and unyielding, even the grass is sharp on their feet. They have been so used to the unreality of their own imaginations, which could be manipulated to their liking that a reality which would not change for their whims was an affront.

That dialectic between liberal and conservative, between truth getting and truth conserving, must be a continual process in the life of the Church. Neither one can override the other. Although we will be majoring in one or the other at any given time, the other will always be there in a healthy community, ready on the back burner to be brought forward when circumstances indicate that to be adviseable.

The Catholic tradition has borne this theme in its teaching of natural theology, insisting that we must use our minds to discover God through the resources of nature around us. The Evangelical tradition at its best likewise has shown a powerful understanding of the need bring the Bible into intellectual confrontation with the world around us. The Anglican tradition has always maintained that along with Scripture as the basis of our doctrine, and community Tradition as the basis for interpreting Scripture, we are committed to the process of finding the truth reasonably (is there any *other* way?).

All three legs of the stool, Scripture, Tradition, and Reason, must be firmly planted on reliable ground, or the stool of Christian faith will have no feet on which to stand. [26] Faith is not a fourth item to add to the three to make a four-legged stool. Rather, faith is what one does *with* the three, namely sit on them. It is the platform on top which unites the legs and makes them useable. Faith means risking the weight of one's being on the evidence of those three legs. Liberal faith is the faith of an Abraham (no less!) who is willing to follow the voice of Truth into the unknown, precisely that through which the content of two legs, Scripture and Tradition, is revealed. Conservative faith is the faith which is willing to rest the weight of one's being on the growing strength of those legs of the stool, on tried and tested truth and on tried and tested means to the truth, a teachable spirit and reasonable inquiry.

---

26 The image of the three-legged stool is, I believe, attributable to Richard Hooker, an Anglican divine of the 16th century.

The Roman part of the Catholic tradition has
sometimes compromised this openness to the truth
with its doctrine of the magisterium and the infallibility of the Pope. Evangelicals have sometimes
compromised this with their doctrines of the infallibility or inerrancy of Scripture. It is difficult to maintain an open inquiring mind in the
atmosphere of "infallibility", for one is seldom
allowed to critically inspect the "infallible"
items. Such inspection becomes a sign of a "lack
of faith" when it may be the very essence of faith.

Liberals, on the other hand, have compromised
their search for the truth by losing sight of the
objective content for which the search aimed in the
first place. Openness-to-the-truth backslides into
emptiness-of-content. It is sometimes difficult to
tell what a liberal means by the word 'Christian'.

On the conservative side, our search for *certainty* (in the guise of infallibility or inerrancy)
can lead us to compromise our search for the *truth*.
But there is no point in being certain about something we do not have reason to hold true. The
conservative quest for external and objective certainty ends then in an ironic turn around, substi-
tuting an inner and somewhat subjective mental
state, infallible certainty, for the objective
truth -- *if* it is not willing to risk its certainty
in the reasonable search for the truth.

The truth would seem to be that there are no
infallible or inerrant items within the created
order. Only God is infallible, who speaks to us
through the many and sundry channels of the creation, but from outside of the created order. It
is only by faith, openness to the truth, that we
come to participate in *His* infallibility *as* we come
to participate in the fullness of His life. Or to
put it more aptly, what we come to participate in
is not so much infallibility as simply -- the truth
-- what is -- as we participate in His life. That
is why Jesus could say that following His commandments would lead into reality, which would set us
free. To be infallible is always a striving and an
effort. To be in truth is to rest in grace.

It is precisely the Biblical sense of an objective truth that frees us to take that open-ended
faith journey into reality. All the more so because of the Christian sense that the truth is
ultimately personal, a Someone, not merely a list
of beliefs or an impersonal universe. This Someone

is Himself calling us into that open and vulnerable encounter with reality where alone we can meet Him. It is only through that open exchange with life and the God of life that knowledge of God becomes, not *infallible*, but increasingly and verifiably *reliable*, something we can stand on and live by.

That gives the Christian community the freedom to "bracket its judgements", to have a genuinely listening spirit, but the freedom likewise to stand firmly on the ground to which it hears God directing it. It gives the Christian community the freedom to deal graciously and inclusively with groups who differ or are even hostile, without compromising the integrity of the truth on which we stand. We can present the truth as God gives it to us, and invite anyone who desires to come join us.

Ultimately, then, exclusion, a conservative sort of activity, happens because there will be those who, for reasons of their own, choose not to have fellowship with that community of revelation.[27] Belonging, after all, has reasonable meaning and content only if there is a possibility of not belonging. That is why there were two special trees in the Garden of Eden, the Tree of Life representing dependency on God with eternal life, and the Tree of the Knowledge of Good and Evil representing independence from God and death. The invitation to openness and inclusiveness, the liberal thrust, is always there, given personal meaning and content precisely because there *is* a potential exclusion. God's invitation is infinitely inclusive, *everyone* is invited. But it is into *His* Kingdom we are invited, not our own. Hell, as someone said, is God's mercy on the unrepentant sinner. God will not force us to live eternally in His presence. He really does give us a choice.

The Christian is called to be a liberal in his search for the truth, but the truth that identifies one as a Christian is a Biblically oriented truth and life style. The legitimate concern for truth must find companionship with a conservative stand-

---

27 C. S. Lewis's book, THE GREAT DIVORCE, vividly portrays the struggle between good and evil, the struggle of judgement, separation, and hell. In a sometimes amusing story of a sight-seeing bus trip from hell up to heaven we witness the spiritual conflict between the two sides. We ultimately reject heaven, and fall, as Leanne Payne says, into the hell of self. As St. John puts it, "And this is the judgement, that the light has come into the world, and men loved darkness rather than light, because their deeds were evil." (3:19)

ing on the given of Revelation. We are called to be liberal in our research and conservative in our conclusions. (That is the tension any honest believer in anything must live with.) The conservative and the liberal are necessary and complementary thrusts (like masculine and feminine) which must remain in dialogue or we will either harden into conservative legalism or dissolve into liberal mush. Wasn't it clever of Satan to strike a cleavage down our center and pit the two sides against each other?

Where openness to the truth and Biblical content cannot live together, there may turn out to be *other* faiths, but there cannot be a *Christian* faith with integrity. Should one conclude that that is indeed the case, should one conclude that the basic fabric of the Biblical worldview and message is not in fact true, then he must follow (and take his chances with) his own conscience. But more honest to be done with the whole thing, including the name 'Christian', than to try to parade what is in fact another religion as Christianity.

The liberals I admired in seminary were those who appeared to me to want to get the truth and live in it, at whatever cost. It was a brave and challenging image. It was the best of the leg of personal experience and reason at work, absolutely necessary for the survival of the Church as a living and saving reality. The contemporary Christian liberal movement, however, has been largely coopted by a very particular and identifiable theological and philosophical position, the "perennial philosophy" described above, which at every point stands mortally opposed to the Biblical faith and experience of life.

For the Christian, launching out on the adventure into truth to know and to live obediently to the God and Father of Jesus Christ is *par excellance* the great romance of life and the adventure of faith.

I I .
I N C L U S I O N   A N D   E X C L U S I O N
T H E   B I B L I C A L   W A Y

Preface

This article, a sequel to the above *Sexuality and Family Life -- The Biblical Roots*, is a response to a report from the Episcopal Diocese of Connecticut dealing with many of the same issues as the report from the Diocese of Newark. The *Connecticut Report*, as we will call it, was issued by the Diocesan Commission on Marriage and Human Sexuality for study and dialogue purposes.

The two reports from Newark and Connecticut show many similar themes and come to some similar conclusions concerning the Christian attitude toward sexual morality. In both instances the reports advocate the liberalization of policy toward homosexual persons, including the writing of liturgies for the marriage of persons of the same sex. Both reports show a similar rejection of the Bible as the source of standards for such matters, and both appeal instead to what they feel is a scientific consensus.

The *Connecticut Report* (to be read in conjunction with the prior "interim report") takes a more conservative stand, however, by upholding marital faithfulness and in not encouraging pre-marital and post-marital sexual relations.

My two responses deal with some similar issues, the secular "perennial" philosophy, the nature of feedom and authority in the Church, and the meaning and relation of gender and sex. The second response, this current article, looks more deeply into the reliance of the two reports on secular science and the roots and meaning of that reliance, and also into the meaning of human nature, particularly with respect to the homosexual question.

My intent is to provide criteria for understanding what might constitute a "Biblical" viewpoint, and an understanding of how a Biblical viewpoint must relate to secularism and to science, matters of great dissention among Christians today.

The prior article contained a full text of the *Newark Report* while the present article relies on quotation in the text to provide background. The full text of the *Connecticut Report* and the "interim report" may be obtained from the diocesan offices at 1335 Asylum Ave., Hartford, Ct., 06105.

A.   "Conflict Resolution" and the *Connecticut Report*

The *Report of the Diocesan Commission on Marriage and Human Sexuality* (hereafter called *The Connecticut Report*), like the similar *Newark Report*, raises issues at stake in nearly every Christian denomination, much of which deals with the broad impact of the secular culture, "secular science" in particular, on the life and message of the Body of Christ. The matters raised reach far beyond Anglican or Episcopal borders and are being hotly debated in the deliberating rooms of every Christian community, and even without the Christian community.

The report represents a great deal of valuable work and effort to inform the people of the Diocese of the problems before us as we work our way through monumental decisions for the life of the Church. It is in the light of that appreciation that I wish to make the following comments which may appear to some to be overly critical, judgemental, or of the "knee jerk" variety. I wish to respond in the spirit of dialogue which the report encourages (p. 38), but dialogue requires frank expression of conviction and opinion as well as willingness to hear the other side out. Issues are the issue, not personalities, and it is the great issues of our time that I wish to address as they are relevant to the content of the report, not criticize personalities. People are more important than ideas, but ideas must nevertheless be openly and frankly shared or our concern for people will also deteriorate. The issues are deeply contested ones with extraordinary impact on the Church and on the nature of the Gospel, and it is therefore very difficult to express one's position with conviction without causing hurt. Hurt will be caused, and we must therefore continually return to the foot of the cross to forgive and be forgiven.

I wish therefore to express thanks to the commission members for their work, and trust that those (on or off the commission) who disagree with my position will try to hear the following comments in a spirit of mutual concern for the truth, for the Lord, and for each other, as I wish to do for theirs. I wish also to renounce any desire to "be right" or to have my way or to have "my side win". Our party line may make us comfortable, but only the truth sets us free.

It does not appear to me, however, that we are involved in a simple rational discussion, such that we can sit around a table and politely discuss the issues in the modern way of applied sociology. "Conflict resolution" and inclusiveness at the level we are facing reaches far deeper to realms of which contemporary sociology knows little. The Church is at war. That we are a polite society (more or less) trying rationally to solve our issues does not change that fact. Modern society errs in thinking that the development of our rational faculties has dispensed with "spiritual warfare" as being primitive and unsophisticated.

On the contrary. The development of our rational faculties has only thrown us into a new and more sophisticated arena within which that same warfare will take place. We enter the intellectual arena at our peril if we do not recognise that. The intellectual struggle for truth is one of the primary battle scenes of that warfare. The modern development of secular and pagan mythologies and the erosion of the rational in western culture ought to make that evident. [1]

The modern bent, not different from the ancient one, is the conviction that our problems are essentially one of education, that if we just learn a little more, sit around and discuss a little more, be polite and courteous to one another, the conflict will go away. If people know the truth, we

1 I can hardly recommend too highly *The Closing of the American Mind*, by Allan Bloom, who focuses on the loss of our grasp of objective truth as the primary cause of the decline of the American (and western) intellectual community. (Simon & Schuster, New York, 1987.)

want to think, they will choose it. No one will willingly and knowingly choose falsehood or evil. We want to "know" our way into the Kingdom, not choose it at the deep level of conversion and repentance.

But the Christian knows that there are ultimate claims upon us from beyond ourselves, and that those claims must be either accepted or rejected. The spiritual warfare is not over intellectual issues so much as over our submission to the presence and will of God. That is, in the final analysis, a matter of choice, not of intellect.

Indeed, a reading of history would compel one to say that most of our human intellectual and cultural and technological efforts have been a monumental effort to ensure that God does not entrude Himself into human affairs. We really want to prove ourselves independent of Him, we really want to show that we do not need His advice or direction, and that we are and of right ought to be free and autonomous beings. In short, the Fall.

The spiritual warfare is simply this: We will use our intellects the more fully and freely and rationally to submit ourselves to God, or we will use them to claim our independence from Him. Either way we will use our intellects. Trusting the wisdom of God rather than our own wisdom does not mean not using our heads. It means recognising that God is smarter than we. That *is* using one's head.

This is not to say that conflict resolution techniques are never appropriate. They indeed are. Some conflicts are caused by misunderstanding and poor communication skills. But such techniques do not resolve the issues of ultimate allegience. They only bring those ultimate issues to bare faced confrontation. Careful and sensitive discussion and development of communication skills at the round table with my opponent may only serve to communicate how indeed we fundamentally disagree.

At that point, the issue is no longer education or exploration of ideas or alternatives, but conversion. One must convert the other, or a third party convert us both, or there will continue ulti-

mate and unresolveable contradiction.[2]   Or
worse, a mishmash compromise of pea soup so that no
clear decisions can be made at all. It is right at
that point that the Christian is called, at any
cost, to stand straight and tall and to speak with
a clear voice and to act on his ultimate loyalties.

B. Pastoral vs. Juridical

The report wants to see itself as fulfilling the
Anglican tradition, and begins immediately with a
quote from another report to the General Convention
of 1973, which the *Connecticut Report* then accepts
"as reasonable and sufficient statements expressing
the Anglican ethos". From the prior report:

> The Anglican tradition has traditionally been more
> interested in, and has manifested its concern with,
> the problems that people's increasing knowledge ex-
> pose them to by a stance of pastoral rather than
> juridical posture. (P. 4)

It is not so stated, but the "juridical" approach is presumeably exemplified by the Roman
Catholic Church in which direction comes clearly
and definitively from the top down. And indeed it
is true that the Anglican approach has shied away
from such definitive statements as the Roman Church
is wont to make. Anglicanism has thereby been
characterized by a much greater measure of individual freedom and ability to explore new issues than
has been the case in the Roman Church, or so it
seems at least from outside the Roman Church. That

---

2 I experienced this in the parish which I pastored from 1971-81. A diocesan mediator
was sent to help resolve certain issues which divided the congregation. It was my
belief that the issues involved the fundmental nature of the Christian faith and
that discussion would probably not lead to "togetherness". The mediator tried the
round table discussion technique, which led to what some of us at least already
knew, that there were fundamental disagreements. We would have to choose whether
Jesus were really to be the center of our life, whether the role of pastor was to
help those who wanted to grow deeply in that life and to keep the channels for that
growth open and clearly marked. It was not, as many wanted to believe, a case of
all moving in the same direction, but simply taking different routes, and why
therefore can we not include everyone. It was a disagreement over the fundamental
direction of movement. There was no way compromise would resolve the issue. We
had to choose.

freedom is one of the key reasons why I have remained in the Episcopal Church at times when I felt it was betraying its identity.

But there has also been a seeming inability of many Anglican bishops and spokesmen to make clear statements about almost any matter, often giving the impression that there is no specific content to Anglican Christianity. One does not gain that impression from reading the *Book of Common Prayer*, which is quite unambiguous in its doctrine and formulations. But despite what we have enshrined time and again in our liturgical formularies, we seem to have an uncanny knack for ignoring all that in order to be "relevant" to the culture around us. That is to say, we want to be "pastoral". J. I. Packer traces much of this mischief to F. D. Maurice of the last century, who, he says, tried to bring the three warring parties (tractarian, evangelical, and broad church) into unity through a watering down of the doctrinal content of their positions. Ignored in his own day, Maurice has become a resource for contemporary efforts to synthesize in practice apparently contradictory theological positions.[3]

The theme of pastoral vs. juridical appears many times:

> Our commitment to the Anglican model for moral decision making - one based on individual responsibility informed by Scripture, tradition, reason, and experience speaks against the legislation of morals. (P. 6.)

> As a result of intolerance, we risk constructing ethics of fear and punishment rather than ethics of love and moral relatedness. (P. 7.)

> Closer to the truth of the matter is that nobody knows when human life with personhood begins. A developmental approach that is open to observable fact and practical experience seems more acceptable than dogmatic certainty. (P. 29.)

> As we delineate the tasks of adolescence.... ...the goal is not the keeping of certain proscriptions, but rather the evolution of an understanding of the place and value of sex in their lives.... The demand upon the Church is that it no longer take a proscriptive stance.... (P. 10.)

---

3 "How Do We Comprehend?", *The Evangelical Catholic*, April 1987, p. 1 ff.

The report quotes Fr. Martin Smith, SSJE:

> Anybody who has cut and dried answers about how the unaffiliated are to live out their sexual relationships, and about which expressions of their sexuality are right or wrong, is unlikely to be really listening or really involved. (P. 17.)

The thrust of the *Connecticut Report*, like the *Newark Report*, is continually to cast traditional morality in the role of the juridical, legalistic, and closed minded authoritarian.

No Christian can argue against a pastoral approach if that term is properly understood. Neither the *Newark Report* nor the *Connecticut Report*, however, give us any explicit guidance as to just how "pastoral" is to be distinguished from "juridical". Yet both reports rest most of the weight of their cases on this distinction.

The quarrel many Christians might have with the Roman way of doing things rests largely on the Roman concept of authority coming solely from the top, buttressed by a doctrine of infallibility. Most of the rest of Christendom does not accept either of these as legitimately binding on the Body of Christ. And the sense of the human race somehow having "outgrown" that kind of paternalism rests to a large extent on the vastly expanded educational systems which are themselves founded on what we have come to know as the "scientific" way of discovering knowledge. It also rests on the Bible having become book a easily accessible to the population. There are no "secrets" anymore. Anyone with an interest and sufficient time and intellect can ask the same questions that at one time only the educated clergy or philosophers could deal with.

The result has been that the "juridical" approach has had to be tempered to deal with the educated laity. But the point of the tempering was that it was assumed that any open minded reading of the Scriptures would produce a fairly consistent agreement among the Body of Christ, that the meaning of the Gospel was reasonably graspable by the ordinary mind. That was why people like John Hus were willing to be burned at the stake to get the Bible into the hands of the common man. It was written *for him*, not for the expert to interpret to him, even though he might need the expert's help at times.

But it was not, I submit, the intention of the Reformers nor of the Anglican divines, nor their expectation, that everyman would become his own infallible pope submitted to no one, nor that the nature of Christian belief would become so problematic that no one would be able to agree as to the nature of the faith, and certainly not that scientific investigation of the Bible would prove its unproveablility. But that is the condition in which we appear to find ourselves today. It was in fact, of course, the warning which the Roman Church issued and why it held to its doctrine of the magisterium of the Church and finally promulgated its doctrine of infallibility just about a hundred years ago. That promulgation was spurred by the long burning and ever hotter fires of the "secular scientific" successes. The Roman mentality does not see that it could be possible for Christian unity to survive the onslaughts of secularism and paganism without the firm hand of Church authority.

The *virtue* of renouncing the Roman type of juridical approach from the Anglican and Reformed point of view was based on the assumption that the truth was fairly clearly stated in Scripture. In our time, however, the virtue of the pastoral vs. the juridical approach is based on quite the *opposite* conclusion, that we are in a sea of ambiguity in which we really cannot look at Scripture and come to any conclusions that could be supported by what we would like to call "scientific methodology". Hence the *Connecticut Report* states:

> We have to acknowledge that there is no consensus within the Church on how Scripture can inform the issues of sexuality and relationship.... We believe that the discussion cannot be held on the level of exegesis.

One must question, therefore, the sense in which the given appeal to a "pastoral" approach really reflects the historic Anglican position.

The report does not wish to abandon Scripture, however, and so:

> To get beyond this impasse it is helpful to meditate on the themes of relationship which span the Biblical texts, specifically those of covenant and Incarnation. (P. 12)

We are not told *how* one is to meditate on the
themes of covenant and Incarnation apart from exegesis of specific texts. It is only from the study
of specific texts that these themes are discovered
in the first place. As both counselor and teacher
I find that progress is made only when one is
forced to get down to specifics. And as I look at
those themes of covenant and Incarnation, they lead
in a direction quite different from that which the
report takes. Biblical folk might have been naive
and unsophisticated compared to us moderns, but
they were quite capable of being clear about what
they thought God was saying to them. And one has
to wonder whether there is such difficulty in exegesis, not because the passages are all that ambiguous, but rather because they say things which
do not coincide with whatever non-Biblical presuppositions the authors have imported into their exegesis. That is an assumption, however, since the
report authors do not give us sufficient specific
material at this point on which one might draw
clear conclusions.

But the matter is not so unclear when one continues to examine the report as to where the presuppositions might be coming from. As one might
suspect, if exegesis is not the basis, if specific
passages are not to be relied upon, then one is
necessarily cast into a rather vague misty region
where other outside influences will fill the vacuum
to supply concrete support to formulate specific
decisions. If the report has specific recommendations, and if the Bible is rejected other than in
vague "thematic" terms, the foundations of those
specific decisions must be coming from elsewhere.

In contrast to the rejection of the juridical,
i.e., the traditional, mode, the report speaks approvingly of "new understandings", "modern knowledge", and "the teachings of Freud" (p. 8), psychology as a "scientific discipline", "scientific
research and method" (p. 19), "recent scholarship"
(p. 21), etc. It seems fairly clear that the bottom line of authority for the authors of the *Connecticut Report* is the weight of what they perceive
as scientific evidence as distinct from the evidence of revelation. In any contest between science and the Bible, science wins.

C. Science vs. the Bible

There was just a few years ago, for those involved at least, an impending conflict which might
have been the Donnybrook of the century, a *coup de
grace* to a perplexing religious myth. A group of
scientists were asked to examine the Shroud of
Turin.[4] The authorities had finally given permission. The array of experts probably equalled or
exceeded anything ever gathered to examine a single
piece of evidence, at least outside of government
or military projects. To a man, from reports
given, the investigators expected scientific evidence to show the shroud to be a fraud or at least
a case of mistaken identity.

And so the forces gathered for battle, once
mighty Revealed Religion versus rampant Secular
Science. The story is worth the reading just for
the sleuthing involved, the extraordinary and
mind-boggling turns of events. The most sophisticated and up to date instruments and techniques
were applied, medical, forensic, chemical, photographic, etc. Never once, not even a single time,
did the evidence ever point to anything but that
this shroud in all probability was indeed the
shroud of Jesus of Nazareth, crucified and risen.
Many of the doubting scientists became believers
resulting from their efforts to disprove. The
bloody battle never took place. The antagonists,
Science and Religion, were last seen smiling, arm
in arm, strolling off into the sunset.

If there was ever a revelation I myself received, it was when I was about seven years old.
My mother had persuaded my then unbelieving father
to read something from the Bible to my year older
brother and me. He chose, of all passages, the
first chapter of Genesis. As he read that passage,
in tones one reserves for things he has the deepest
respect for but does not believe, the whole panora-
ma of creation unfolded before me. I do not recall
his ever reading another word of Scripture to us
again, but that was all it took. From that moment
on, it was perfectly clear to me that God had created everything. I could not later understand why
people saw a conflict between science and religion,
why they thought science had somehow disproven re-

---

4 See *Verdict on the Shroud*, by Kenneth E. Stevenson and Gary R. Habermas, Dell/Ban-
bury, Wayne, Pa., 1987. There are many other accounts of this event available.

ligion. It was perfectly clear to me that God had
created science. How can the creature disprove the
Creator?

Be that as it may, the current perception of the
situation is that science, or scientific methodology, has had the effect of seriously undermining our
ability to believe in traditional religion. We
would do well seriously to study just what this
entity called "science" is all about. In just what
sense has it really been successfully used to disprove the claims of the Gospel or of the Biblical
worldview?

Throughout the *Connecticut Report*, the impression is given of a naive and uncritical acceptance
of the findings of "science", as though there were
a body of scientifically unchallenged evidence both
in general and on the specific matters at issue.
Anyone familiar with the history of science must be
aware of the fact that that history is littered
from end to end with discarded theories once
thought to be chiseled in eternal granite.

In a technological sense we are most certainly
acquiring a vast body of knowledge about many
things. But in a philosophical sense, the realm of
science is in anything but a stable state of affairs. I, as did most of us, grew up a "Newtonian"
during the 1940's because the world of hard, massy
atoms moving through space was what the culture
popularly believed to be true. By the '50's, relativity physics, which tells us that time and space
have no privileged anchor points or center points
and that all such "privilege" is strictly relative
to the viewpoint of the observer, had begun to hit
the popular imagination, so far as it is imaginable. And then we heard the mysteries of quantum
mechanics, which implies that we cannot be sure
that an atom or electron really exists out there
until we perceive it, with which even Einstein had
problems.

The pursuit of the atom, the smallest bit of
whatever there is, seemed to be leading into an
endless plummeting downward into more and more ab-
struse and problematic entities and into a world
that no one is sure even exists. These were each
not merely bumps in the road, but major shocks in
what we had hoped to be the steady move forward
into an increasingly rational truth. The objective
world seemed to be disintegrating out from under
us.

70

If one is looking to science, therefore, as a philosophical support for much of anything, he is in for a rude awakening, for the philosophy of science is currently having great difficulty explaining how it is even on a quest for knowledge of an objective reality. Truth, if by that one means some rational explanation of what life is all about, has not at all been forth coming from the laboratories and think tanks of secular science. On the contrary, we are exeriencing a steady erosion of the sense of an objective world out there. What was once the bastion of objective truth, the old Newtonian view, has given place to a view of truth that is, and must be by its own presuppositions, increasingly sliding into subjectivism and solipsism, the view that only I exist and that all the world is my personal creation. A recent issue of *Discover*, a magazine meant to translate some of the more recent movements of the scientific community into popular language, had for a cover article, "A 'What You See is What You Beget' Theory", suggesting what Werner Heisenberg had already gotten the ball rolling on years before with his particular interpretation of quantum physics, that somehow our perceiving of a thing is what creates it.[5] Philosophically we are moving pell mell into subjectivism. Much of pop religion in the so-called "New Age Movement" is heavily into subjectivism and solipsism.

If one looks to mathematics, which surely deals with objective truth (2+2 always does equal 4, doesn't it?), for consolation, there too he will be disappointed, for a mathematician by the name of Kurt Gödel has proven to the satisfaction of most other mathematicians that we cannot prove that 2+2=4.[6] That is (if I understand the matter correctly), mathematical proofs or number theory are somewhat of the nature of geometry. The proofs of geometry rely upon axioms which themselves are not

5 *Discover*, May 1987, p. 90 ff. The article develops some of the implications of Einstein's theory of relativity and of the theory of indeterminacy coming out of quantum mechanics.
See Heisenberg's *Physics and Philosophy*, Harper Bros., New York, 1958, for a fairly readable account of quantum physics and its implications for the reality of an objective physical world.

6 If you are mathematically enclined, you might tackle Gödel himself: *On Formally Undecidable Propositions*, Basic Books, New York, 1962.
Also see *Mathematics - The Loss of Certainty*, by Morris Klein, Oxford University Press, New York, 1980.

geometrically proveable and therefore are arbitrarily imported from outside of geometry to create different kinds of geometry (Euclidean, Reimannian, straight space, curved space, closed space, open space, etc). Mathematics, if it is proveable at all, is at least not mathematically proveable.

Everywhere we look we find ourselves being pushed back to mysterious basic assumptions which themselves are not proveable, other than by the fact that they are indispensible for us to make sense out of anything else.

*   *   *   *

Both the *Newark* and the *Connecticut Report* reflect our times in their reliance upon "science" to provide us with the basic substance of our beliefs. To be "scientific" is assumed to be "true". But there is no such entity as monolithic "science" in the often supposed notion, such that it can make pronouncements on truth or falsehood. There are only many and varied scientists trying, more or less successfully, to use a *method* which is scientific.

Scientific method is not anything mysterious. It is what we all do every day in a rough and ready form. Scientific method is common sense honed to a fine edge. What we call "science" when we say that "science says...." is simply the often very precarious current agreement on certain issues that might obtain at a given time. What "science" says has proved to be somewhat changeable, so that it behooves us to take "science" with a grain of salt.

And in any case, it is not proper for us to look to science for the basic presuppositions of life, for scientific method itself relies upon presuppositions coming from outside of itself. We need to know, in any given case of "scientific" declaration, just what the presuppositions behind the declaration might be. For it is becoming very evident that every scientific enterprise carries with it a burden of philosophical and theological import, particularly obvious in matters of psychology and sociology.

After seminary in the late '50's, I spent three and a half years writing my doctoral thesis at Oxford University on the relation between science and theology. Oxford was then one of the world centers of positivist philosophy, the logical place to go should one desire to test the Christian religion against the philosophical currents of the times. I had known that things philosophically speaking were not very healthy for the human race. We now look back on the '50's as the "healthy" decade, but that was only the relative calm between World War II of the '40's and the descent into the chaos of the '60's and '70's, and now the '80's. We were already in the '50's quite literally running out of meaning.

As Allen Bloom shows in his excellent book, *The Closing of the American Mind*, our current plight had its roots as early as the beginnings of what we thought was the "enlightenment". But neither science nor scientific method, with which Christians have no argument, had brought us to this plight. The culprit was the *secularizing* of science. The secular worldview, one form of the so-called "perennial philosophy", treats the cosmos as though God did not exist or as though He were essentially irrelevant.

The basic tenets of the perennial philosophy are (1) that the cosmos is itself the divine or enduring or substantial entity of the universe, the cosmos is in effect God, (2) that truth is essentially relative, not objective, (3) that morality is likewise a relative matter, not objective, (4) that the way to the divine or ultimate reality involves abandoning the use of the intellect, and (5) that autonomy and self-sufficiency are our primary and fundamental goals so that the pursuit of the divine intails abandoning relationship as well as intellect. Each of these beliefs is in clear evidence in every aspect of western culture. And each of them is in clear contradiction to the Biblical faith. The five points constitute a check list by which we can test any position to tell whether it is a candidate for the Biblical framework.[7]

Secular minded people quickly took hold of this new interest in empirical science (e.g. in the renaissance, the French revolution, the enlightenment) thinking that it effectively established their case by focusing our search for truth on the world itself rather than on a God beyond the world. But now that things have run their course, if my perceptions above are correct, we find that the

---

7 I have written more fully on the Perennial Philosophy in a book to be available early in 1988, *Yahweh or the Great Mother? -- Man and Woman in the Image of God*. See endnote on Emmaus Ministries for details.

search for truth in the world always leads right back out of it again. We are always bumping into "ultimate presuppositions" of which we know not what in the world to make. And since we are not very willing to look out of the world, we give up and rest on the totally untenable position that it really is all relative anyhow, we are just floating on a sea of something-I-know-not-what,[8] unaware that the I-Know-Not-What has chosen to reveal Himself to us as very definitive and concrete I AM. We may not know who He is, but He does, and He is trying to tell us. One is reminded of St. Paul's remarks:

> Where is the wise man? Where is the scribe? Where is the debater of this age? Has not God made foolish the wisdom of the world? (I Cor. 1:20)

It became evident in my researches through the history of the philosophy of science that the roots of the disintegration of our grasp on objective reality go back to even before the time of Newton. His successors, Locke, Hume, Berkeley, and Kant raised questions, not only about God and religion, but about scientific procedure itself and about knowledge of the objective world, questions which were never answered, resulting in our current massive descent into subjectivism.

It also became evident that the mysterious abyss of nothingness and meaninglessness which had been slowly opening up within western civilization, and which was increasingly becoming a central theme in art, music, and literature, was due to our having abandoned the very roots of the scientific worldview, namely the Biblical framework. Christians gave the scientific enterprize away to the enemy, an avowedly Godless world, and are paying a horrendous price for having done so. Scientific method is one of the most finely honed edges of the Sword of the Spirit, the word of Truth. We laid it neatly in the lap of the enemy, who then proceeded to put the edge to our throat. Smart, huh?

---

8 See "Before the Big Bang: The Big Foam", *Discover*, September 1987, p. 76 ff. Ultimate creation is pictured as a total chance event: "In answer to the question of why it happened, I offer the modest proposal that our Universe is simply one of those things which happen from time to time." The attempt to find ultimate meaning or rational explanation is abandoned. The suggestion that a theological answer might supply the missing rationality is not considered.

My work was devoted to proving on philosophy's own grounds (the grounds of common sense) that the scientific enterprize necessarily presupposed the existence of a Biblical type God. In other words, all those blind alleys that Heisenberg and Gödel and others seem to lead us down are actually pointing us back to the primary roots of western civilation, roots to which we had laid the axe, the God of Abraham, Isaac, and Jacob. A personal, living God is the ultimate "axiom", if you like, without which life makes no sense, not even scientific sense.[9] It simply is not true that science or scientific method operates on its own, on a kind of neutral ground, independently of deep philosophical and theological commitments.

Science does keep on working with or without the scientist's belief in God, bridges keep getting built, we get to the moon, but *there has been given from the secular standpoint no adequate explanation as to why science and technology work*. Not only geometry and number theory, but the cosmos itself has ultimate presuppositions which must be assumed if we are to make any rational sense of it all. We, the human race, were all so busy looking in the wrong direction that the Ultimate Presupposition had to come to reveal Himself in person. We are no longer facing the question, -- Given the obvious brute fact of the world, can we prove (or do we even need) the existence of God? Rather, we are facing the question, -- Now that we have chosen to go without God, can we rescue (or do we even need!) the existence of the world?

It rankles the modern sensibilities to be told that the ultimate presupposition of life is a personal Creator God, and not an abstract theory or law, like $E=MC^2$, or $2+2=4$. Philosophers of science are straining after what they call a "unified field theory", a single comprehensive law which overarches all others, uniting relativity physics, quantum mechanics, thermodynamics, electromagnetics, and anything else. To say that a *Person* is behind all this appears silly and worthy of contempt to the current way of thinking. To say that persons, not

9 I expect to have a book ready for distribution early in 1988, *Personality, Empiricism, and God*, which develops this argument, based on my work at Oxford. (See end note on Emmaus Ministries.)

  Others have already written on the subject. See especially Stanley Jaki, *Science and Creation*, Scottish Academic Press, 1974, Edinburgh. Also Gordon H. Clark, *The Philosophy of Science and Belief in God*, The Craig Press, Nutley, N.J., 1974.

things, are the basic building blocks of the universe, persons, not electrons, protons, quarks, or
snarks, or any of the more esoteric entities continually being discovered, and to say that this is
the only *rational* way to look at life, is likely to
bring stupified silence, or condescension about the
"religious" way of looking at things.[10] It is
nevertheless the case that I believe can be made.
If it cannot, then Christians will always be labor-
ing under a sense of being out of touch with reality and under a niggling sense of inferiority in the
presence of "science".

I do not wish to suggest that the *Connecticut
Report* has no roots in the Bible, but there is a
clear drift away from the Bible toward a source of
revelation whose track record is philosophically
and theologically (as against technologically) not
very impressive. Secular science has provided us
neither with an explanation of ultimate sources nor
with a perception of ultimate goals. That is OK.
We should not have thought it could. But also we
should not be abandoning our own Biblical heritage
which is the only way we can establish a rational
sense of an ultimate source and a perception of
ultimate goals, and thereby provide those ultimate
presuppositions upon which all science and all rationality are ultimately based.

The sense in which the report reflects a uniquely Christian view is very unclear. The alleged
scientific data or theory to which it refers may or
may not be valid. That is a matter for deeper
investigation. The facts, if there be such, will
have to stand on their own feet. That is the Biblical way of truth seeking. But facts stand in a
philosophical and theological framework, and they

_____

10 I feel it safer to hide discretely in a footnote the following statement, that Jesus
already gave us the only really "unified field theory" that will work, and that any
unified field theory that occurs in nature will have to be subsumed under this one:
"You shall love the Lord your God with all your heart, and with all your soul, and
with all your mind. This is the great and first commandment. And a second is like
it, You shall love your neighbor as yourself. On these two commandments depend all
the law and the prophets." (Mt. 22:34 ff.)
      The law and the prophets for Jesus of course were the basic Hebrew Scriptures,
the account of creation and of revelation history. By implication Jesus was saying
that this law (or two laws) sum up the meaning of the cosmos, implying that all
law, all the created order, including natural law, is here to fulfill this primary
and over arching law of love. Nature, including its laws, was put here to provide
a stable and reliable stage or platform or arena in which a community of love can
be built, the Kingdom of heaven.

stand under the judgement of the purpose of existence implied or given in that framework. It is at
this point that the *Connecticut Report* appears deficient. One would like to be able to assume that
a report written by a Christian committee could be
assumed to be rooted in the Bible. But in a culture as much at odds with itself as ours, with so
little consensus even within the Church as to what
is "Biblical", in a culture so contentedly "pluralistic", one can no longer assume anything. We need
to see it spelled out, in clear and specific terms.

But it is precisely at the point of clarity and
precision that the report wants to shy away. Persons who have a clear and precise sense of morality
are apparently suspected of legalism, rigidity,
"cut and dried" answers. I would submit that the
issue is not whether a reponse is cut and dried or
whether it is legalistic, but first of all whether
it is true. No doubt we have all been the victims
of persons who tried to stuff us into boxes into
which we did not fit. But we have also no doubt
all been guilty of avoiding issues that we did not
want to face and used the cry of "unfair!" to get
our way.

One does not wish to pit Christian moral tradition against the truth. One does not wish to find
himself in the position of holding an outdated tradition in the face of clearly established facts.
If it should turn out that the Bible is indeed
proven wrong or inadequate on a point, such as the
acceptability of sexual relations outside of marriage or homosexual relations, then we will just
have to deal with that realistically and with charity. But we are not obligated to listen to some
entity called "science" as though it has the last
word on a subject. We are more interested in
whether a statement is *true* than whether it is
"scientific". And the two are not necessarily syn-
onymous. The issues of science to which the report
refers are in some cases fairly recent, and in *no*
case are they unanimously agreed upon within the
scientific community. But one would not know that
from a reading of the report.

Many of the presuppositions of the *Connecticut
Report* would appear to come from the very secularized science that has on a massive scale replaced
the Biblical worldview and its values. And even if
certain factual data of the traditional approach
were found to be faulty, if we are yet to retain

our Christian identity, we are obliged to interpret
those facts from within that framework of basic
presuppositions which gives us our identity. We
will be dealing with some of those items more
specifically.

D. The Secular Root

Secularism did not spring fully formed at some
point in western history. The strength of Christian tradition was too deeply rooted. Secularism
has lived, by and large, on the capital generated
by that Biblical tradition at whose roots it has so
furiously hacked. As the pieces of that tradition
were slowly eroded by the negative forces at work,
so did secularism erode in its own ability to
appear to give viable answers to the human situation. It was western culture's rerun of the Fall.

Ironically, but appropriately enough, the erosion of that ability comes precisely with the
appearance of the five characteristics listed above
of the perennial philosophy. Each one of those
five characteristics is an enemy of rational inquiry. Any movement within the Christian fold to
lean on those five "broken reeds" will only betray
our efforts as Christians to meet the needs of a
broken world. And yet a great deal of contemporary
Christian thinking does indeed so rely.

The *first characteristic* of the perennial philosophy is its identification of God or the divine
with the cosmos. We experience the "otherness" of
God primarily through our dependency on Him as
source of our being and welfare, and through our
submission and obedience to His will. The Old Testament Hebrew experience of the will of God bringing order out of chaos, giving them a law which
could form them into a unique and special people,
correcting them and judging them, came long before
any developed theology of God being their Creator
ex nihilo. The sense of the moral leadership of
God and His claim in their lives issuing out of the
promise to Abraham and the Exodus and Mount Sinai
experience were the beginning foundation of their
sense of the majesty and lordship of God.

When we lose the sense of the will of God as a specific and determinable influence in our lives, we soon lose the sense of the distinction of God apart from the cosmos at all. A God who has no will and purpose for us has little impact on our lives. The personal nature of God is unsupportable apart from the experience of the will of God. Persons, human or divine, are in their very essence purposive, willing beings. A God without ultimate and overriding purpose is no God at all. Significantly, will and purpose are typically at the masculine end of the masculine-feminine spectrum, a matter which we will explore more fully. It is the masculine side of the divine that has fallen into disrepute in our time.

It should be no surprise to find that in the secular world, universal or cosmic purpose is not to be found. There are only the individual purposes of individual persons, or at best groups that are able to form together in common purpose. But there is no overarching purpose by which all other purposes are judged.

The *Connecticut Report* certainly does not explicitly deny the Biblical otherness of God, and it gives us some healthy direction in urging the acceptance of our sexual nature as God's gift to us in His image (p. 6-8). But this primary experience of the will of God is not much in evidence. The Bible, as the traditional expression of that will for over 20 centuries, is held to be inadquate to convey that will to us in our time, with the resultant appeal to empirical science apparently as the last court of appeal.

Clearly a loving God will not command us to do something that we literally cannot do. God will not contradict Himself by creating something and then giving it a purpose contrary to its abilities. So we can indeed learn something about the will of God by looking at the creation. If I am *by divinely given nature* constituted a homosexual, then only a malevolent God would order me to behave otherwise. But the *will* of God under which our actions might be held in judgement does not appear as a central consideration in the report. The appeal is consistently to certain empirical studies concerning the facts of behavior, facts which seem to be taken as a basis for forming a moral judgement.

The report does not point us unambiguously to a place of judgement coming from *outside* the created order.

The practical effect of this is to collapse God into the cosmos, for the will of God is discovered *only* by studying the cosmos, not also by listening to God.

The *second characteristic* of the perennial philosophy, increasingly evident in secular thinking, is that there is no objective truth, that truth is by nature subjective, and relative only to oneself.

In the October 1987 issue of *Good News*, the Connecticut diocean newspaper, appeared an excellent article on efforts to use advertizing techniques to inform people of the Good News. The cover of *Good News* had an example of their work. The head caption of the piece was:

> In a World of Easy Answers, It's Nice to Know People With Questions.

And then the text below a picture of a woman praying:

> Perhaps the easy answers to life's hardest questions aren't the ones you're seeking. Come join a group of men and women who struggle, just as you do, with the hard questions of life. And who know that there aren't any easy answers.

The piece is clearly reaching out to a need of our times, to people who have retreated from the glib and facile. But one also wants to say, perhaps not on this particular piece, but somewhere loudly and clearly, that there are *real* answers and *reliable* answers. We may not have them all here in this life, but God knows what He is doing, and we can trust that in due time the answers will be given to us. In the meantime, there are answers that we can trust sufficiently to base our life on them and to move forward positively.

Life is not a dull plodding into the grey unknown, and the consolation of the Christian faith is not simply that we have a few others with whom to share the tragic truth that there are no answers. There is a reliable Truth that will set us free, and we have the Good News of Him to share. The accepted theological pluralism (p.4) of the report suggests a slim hold on this primary foundation.

Ted Koppel, anchorman of ABC-TV's "Nightline", commented in his commencement address to the seniors at Duke University in May 1987:

In the place of truth, we have discoverd facts. For moral absolutes, we have substituted moral ambiguity. We now communicate with everyone and say absolutely nothing. We have reconstructed the Tower of Babel, and it is a television antenna: a thousand voices producing a daily parody of democracy, in which everyone's opinion is afforded equal weight, regardless of substance or merit.[11]

The above leads directly to the *third characteristic*, that moral truth also is relative.

The report does not embrace such a position directly, but does affirm the position of a report to General Convention (quoted on page 4) that this report "reflects our recognition of the reality of theological and ethical pluralism."[12]

This reference to ethical and theological pluralism might be an innocuous reference to the fact which has always been true in the Church that there are divergent opinions about many matters. In the following paragraph the report explicitly rejects, as any Christian would, ethical relativism or a totally individualized approach (p. 5).

But it remains nevertheless that the substance of our theological pluralism is in many instances strongly influenced by the contemporary sense of there being no objective truth. All this is cutting right at the heart of what has been understood for centuries to be the center of the Christian faith, in particular the Bible as the foundation of doctrine, and the theology of Incarnation, cross, resurrection, and the Trinity as the primary creedal foundation stones.

There has been a mode of interpretation of basic texts, which in naked form seems so ridiculous that few would embrace it, called "deconstructionism", which Allan Bloom calls

the last, predictable, stage in the suppression of reason and the denial of the possibility of truth in the name of philosophy. The interpreter's creative activity is more important than the text, there is no text, only interpretation. Thus the one thing

---

11 Reprinted in *The Noel News*, November/December 1987, p. 11.

12 See section B above, "Pastoral vs. Judicial".

most necessary for us, the knowledge of what these texts have to tell us, is turned over to the subjective, creative selves of these interpreters, who say that there is both no text and no reality to which the texts refer.[13]

It is this same treatment of our Constitution which has led to the current position on the wall of separation between Church and State, which is not in the Constitution, and by any fair reading of history was not in the minds of those who wrote it. It is in the minds of those who want to "interpret" it for us in the light of prevailing secular pluralistic philosophy. Plural less one -- the traditional mainstream Biblical viewpoint.

Again, the *Connecticut Report* hardly embraces such a position, but it is at the same time difficult to see what would prevent it from sliding in that direction when it is unable to find specific texts in Scripture to exegete and is willing to rest the formulation of Christian moral standards on the foundations of avowedly pagan and secular interpreters of reality.[14] It is difficult to distinguish between the "pluralism" which they find acceptable and the "relativism" which they do not. The only way to make such a distinction clear is to have identifiably clear moral principles -- from which the report shies away.

The report refers to the "responsible Christian" (p. 5) in admirable terms with which few would quarrel, excepting that something is left out. As in the *Newark Report*, there is a consistent absence of the masculine side of the gender spectrum in favor of the feminine side, not that the feminine side should be absent, but rather that it should be appropriately wedded to the masculine:

> When we speak of the "responsible" Christian, however, we must avoid such relativism, recognizing it as incompatible with the Gospel. As the Gospel reveals a forgiving, healing, self-sacrificing, compassionate Christ, the Christian labors in the process of decision making in this context. (p. 5.)

---

13 *The Closing of the American Mind*, p. 379.

14 See below, section H, "The Poisoned Well".

The missing element is Christ as judge, direction giver, and Lord. We do indeed labor in the context mentioned, but we also labor in the context of the will of God for His creation. *We* are busy making decisions, seemingly unaware that *God* has already made decisions to which we are to conform. The report to General Convention quoted affirms likewise that sheer individualism is not a proper response for Christians:

> It is becoming clear that the principle issue is not the rightness of any individual action judged by the immediate circumstance, but the proper assumption of responsibility for decisions made in relation to the facts as they can be known at any given time and with proper regard for the quality of life possible for all humankind at all time... (p. 4.)

But again the missing element. The word 'responsible' is used in an ambiguous manner. On one hand it can refer to the fact that I am responsible for my decisions, meaning simply that I admit to what I decide. I "take responsibility" for doing something. That kind of responsibility is necessary for any moral response, but by itself it is not yet a *moral* response.

On the other hand the word 'responsibility' gains a moral connotation by indicating that I am responsible *to* someone. 'Responsibility' has no moral sense if it is not specified *to whom* I am responsible. There must be someone to whom I am to respond. I am respons-able, that is to say, accountable. Morality always implies an authority under which I stand. But if the will of God has been factored out of the situation, then the essential Person, the One Who Decides my purpose for existence, to whom I am to respond, is no longer a meaningful factor, and the moral element disappears. To be a *Christian* moral response, it is not sufficient merely to be concerned for the facts of a case and for the "quality of life", any secular or pagan person can do that. One must also be a disciple of (disciplined by) Jesus. Gentle Jesus, meek and mild, has backbone:

> My food is to do the will of Him who sent me, and to accomplish His work.

> If you continue in my word, you are truly My disciples, and you will know the truth, and the truth will set you free. (John 4:34, 8:31)

Jesus has a word for us directly from the Father, we are to continue in it, and doing so will lead us to the real truth of life, not just to someone's "interesting interpretation". That, and nothing less, will set us free.

Ted Koppel to the Duke University graduating class again:

> And gradually, it must be said, we [TV] are be-ginning to make our mark on the American people. We have actually convinced ourselves that slogans will save us. Shoot up, if you must, but use a clean needle. Enjoy sex whenever and with whomever you wish, but wear a condom.
> "No." The answer is "No". Not because it isn't cool or smart or because you might end up in jail or dying in an AIDS ward, but "no" because it's wrong, because we have spent 5,000 years as a race of ra-tional human beings, trying to drag ourselves out of the primeval slime by searching for truth and moral absolutes.[15]

The *fourth characteristic* of the perennial phi-losophy is its insistance that the royal road to the divine entails the divestiture of our intellec-tual capacities, that since the merely human mind is not capable of grasping the divine, we must approach God through pure experience devoid of propositional content. The Biblical view is that there are certainly non-intellectual, non-proposi-tional aspects of our faith which are central and necessary. But the Bible will also insist that there are things about God which are true and which can indeed be known to be true because God has Himself chosen to make them known, and that the propositional and the non-propositional are both relating us to the same basic reality which is a personal God, and are therefore complementary and mutually supportive..

The *Connecticut Report* does not tell us that feelings or experiences are to be valued at the expense of intellectual perception. But the lack of intellectual clarity, the tendency toward plu-ralism, and the suspicion of anyone who claims to have any clear answers prompts one to wonder how the authors of the report would resist that tenden-cy to rely on feelings and experience at the ex-pense of the intellectual and propositional. I am not suggesting that the experiential or feeling or

---

15 *The Noel News*, November/December, p. 11.

intuitive should be crammed into an intellectual framework unfit for them. I am suggesting that none of these can pull rank over the other, that each must be allowed its contribution, and that so long as they do not agree, we need to keep working on all of them until they do come into agreement. Truth itself is not split apart, only our muddled approaches to it, or to Him.

Likewise concerning the *fifth characteristic*, the report does not explicitly campaign for human self-sufficiency and autonomy. But there is a kind of individualism in the report which is inherent in its consistent rejection of the authority role of the Church, which is neither characteristic of Biblical culture, nor does it proceed logically from Biblical principles in which submission to Godly and civil authority is expected. So it has to be coming from another source. This individualism comes out most clearly in the discussion concerning the "responsible Christian", who is not held to be responsible *to* anyone outside of himself. Church authorities are to be "pastoral", not "juridical", they are to offer advice, guidance, and encouragement, but not "coerce" a decision with a threat of punishment. Any hint of "consequences" for behavior appears to be considered coercive and oppressive:

> Ultimately, each (person) makes his or her own decision, and the Church can only provide the support necessary to allow them to arrive at those decisions in keeping with their informed consciences with the least possible civil constraint consistent with the peace and safety of all of the people. (p. 4, from the report to General Convention.)

No one wants governmental interference or Church hierarchy meddling in one's private affairs, but this is being interpreted in such a manner as to make us self-contained units morally speaking, listening only to our own consciences. One wonders if there is to be any point at all at which the Church is to be able to say, "No, you may not do that and remain in communion with us as a Christian body." The point at which one says "no" is as determinative as the point at which one says "yes" in establishing one's identity boundaries.

It appears to be assumed that we are all rational enough and committed enough to make moral decisions apart from accountability to some other person or body, that our consciences are informed by
the voice of God, and that there are no significant
spiritual or cultural counter-forces at work which
might intrude themselves and destroy the processes
of soul saving and community building. The need
for disciplinary action is not seen. I have to
believe that this is due to the strong drift in the
Church into nihilistic relativism, dressed up as
inclusive pluralism. Much of this is done in the
name of togetherness and inclusiveness and community, but the kind of individualism fostered is in
fact making that very community an impossibility.
A community that as a matter of principle cannot
say "no" has lost its integrity. For the very
boundaries of identity, not only of a person but
also of a community, are defined by its "yes" and
its "no".

The tendency to reduce accountability in the
interests of a pastoral approach have the effect of
emphasizing feelings and pleasure at the expense of
objective standards. Feelings become the standard
by which rightness and wrongness is judged. For
all the desire for inclusiveness, when one retreats
into feelings apart from an objectively accountable
relationship, one ends up tending to include others
only insofar as they make him feel good, not for
any value (objective) of their own. And so the
whole project turns on its head, producing exactly
the opposite of what it originally aimed at, and
only confirms the fifth characteristic, autonomy
and self-sufficiency at the expense of objectivity,
i.e. at the expense of relationship.

A book was written several years ago in which
the author said that the most important thing on
earth is "looking out for Number One". The book
was "dedicated to the hope that somewhere in our
universe there exists a civilization where the inhabitants possess sole dominion over their own
lives."[16] There is a clear thrust in contemporary society toward building a society where I will
be accountable to no authority but my own. Unfor-
tunately there is already such a place. It is
called hell, the place where people have totally
divorced themselves from the claim of God upon

16 This was gleaned from a pamphlet, "Power for Living", put out by the American Tract
Society, Box 462008, Garland, TX 75046.

their lives. "Better to reign in hell than to
serve in heaven!" says Satan in Milton's *Paradise
Lost*, one of the great "heroic" lines of all time.

E. Sex and Gender in Creation

One of the most difficult aspects of our current
Church culture for me to understand is our headlong
rush into monumental changes in doctrine and practice when at the same time we have next to no
theological foundation and no consensus in those
areas of change. The solution for most of our current issues must rely on a deep understanding of
sexuality and gender and human nature and divine
nature, all of which are divisive issues among us.
We have no accepted theology of sexuality at all,
and nearly no theology of the priesthood, or at
least no consensus on it. And yet we have made far
reaching changes in our ordination policy by the
inclusion of women, we are in the process of
de-sexing our liturgical texts, and we are considering radically altering our sexual moral commitments, all related issues. This sort of behavior
cannot but come from a pulling rank of instinct,
intuition, and gut feeling over serious thinking
about a problem.

I have asked many times of groups or individuals, when the question of the relation between sex
and gender came up, "What is your definition of
'masculine' or 'feminine'?" Never once has there
ever come back a clear answer. Almost universally
there is a blank look. Often, especially when I
suggest that the definition of 'masculinity' has to
do with spiritual authority, the response comes
back, "I do not think we need those words any more.
They probably do not have any meaning." I suspect,
though I do I do not know for sure, that there is
galloping through the back of their minds the uneasy thought, "I wonder what the feminists will
think of my answer?" They have no sure intellectual footing to understand the issues, and they have
the enormous emotional weight of cultural feminism
staring at them. And at that point, I think, most
people simply give up.

Dictionary definitions of the two words tend to offer something like, "behavior appropriate to a male/female", leaving to the reader to decide what constitutes "appropriate". The matter is left to the cultural relativists to decide.

The feminist approach has become so much a part of the assumptions of our culture that it is only with difficulty that some crucial issues can be raised anymore. No doubt that is the way the feminists felt a few years ago, maybe still do. One hesitates to raise the issues of women's ordination, for example, not only because one does not like to get verbally shot at, but also because, we having launched into the enterprise, there are many persons of one's own acquaintance who are deeply and personally committed into the venture. The amount of hurt and pain that can emerge out of such an open discussion is more than most of us want to deal with. It means opening up again the question of whether we made the right decision in 1976 to admit women to ordination, and consideration of the possibility, however remote, of having to turn the ship around. Even those who disagree with the 1976 decision are aware of the anguish many women in particular would have to endure, were that to happen.

It is situations like these that make me think of Jesus' statement that, if we are faithful to His commandments as His disciples, we will find the truth, and the truth will set us free (John 8:31 ff.), as the most daring and outrageous statement of faith anywhere to be found. Jesus is saying that we must, in His company, risk the hurt and pain and alienation and loneliness to just get at the truth, whatever it is. That risk to be open to the truth is the essential risk of faith. Following Jesus is a discipleship in living in the truth, at any cost.

With that in mind, I venture the following thoughts on the nature of gender and sexuality. These thoughts are more fully expressed elsewhere and here will be given only a hint of the extraordinary scope of the possibilities.[17] I believe that the confusion of our times in these areas rest

---

17 I expect to have a much more complete work available early in 1988, *Yahweh or the Great Mother? - Man and Woman in the Image of God*, developing a basis for a full scale Biblical psychology. Currently available is an album of 12 cassette tapes building this case. See end note on Emmaus Ministries for further details.

on some basic errors of understanding in Biblical theology, and that the Bible has its own unique picture of gender and sex relations, the roots of which are right in the account of creation, Genesis 1 and 2. My hope is that coming to understand this picture will help lead us through the turmoil ahead into a solid and peaceful acceptance of one another and of the extraordinary, powerful, and unique gifts that we have to offer each other as men and women.

* * * * *

Three concepts basic to all life need to be clarified briefly in order to understand the meaning of the issues of masculinity and femininity, authority, power, and freedom. If asked the meaning of authority, people will often answer something like, "that is when someone else is in control of your life". Power will be generally seen as "the ability to get your way in the circumstances around you". And freedom will be the ability to "do your own thing". Seen in that light, being under authority and having freedom are antithetical, and there is little distinction between authority and power, both being aimed at "getting my way".

But suppose authority is defined as "the freedom to do that for which you exist". And suppose power is seen as "the ability to be myself", the power of being. Authority, then, has to do with doing, whereas power has to do with being. And neither have to do with license to get my way.

In Genesis 1:26 ff., we read that God decided to create the human race in His own image, to give us dominion over the rest of creation, and that being created "in His image" means specifically being created male and female. Since God is not a biological being, He is neither male nor female. He is not biologically a sexual being. But the passage does indicate that our being biological sexual beings is a reflection of something that was already in His nature before there were any of us around. Since God is a spiritual being, those qualities of which our sexuality is a reflection must themselves be spiritual qualities.

The only qualities that present themselves to mind are those of masculinity and femininity, qualities which are much broader and at the same time reach much deeper than the literal biological qualities. Manhood, then, or physical maleness, is in some sense an image, or reflection, or sacrament of the spiritual quality of masculinity in God. And then womanhood, or physical femaleness, is likewise an image, or reflection, or sacrament of the spiritual quality of femininity in God.

I wish to draw a distinction between sex as the physical, biological, genital aspect of our nature and gender as the much broader qualities which far transcend literal physical sexuality. We understand gender terms in relation to many things and events that have no literal sexual reference at all. In this sense, God has no sex, for He is not a physical, biological being. But gender as a spiritual quality might well be a part of the divine nature. Without this distinction, it would seem impossible to make any sense of the Genesis passage which tells of our being made male and female in the image of God.

The existence of a feminine element in God has been much debated, with the conservative branch generally dissenting and the liberal branch affirming. I do not see that we have a choice in the matter, for there does not appear to be any other way to read the Genesis text as it stands. Moreover, there are many instances throughout Scripture of God behaving in a very feminine manner (see for example, Isaiah 66:7-13).

One of the Old Testament names for God, El Shaddai, has a root meaning of "many breasted God". The name also has the meaning of "almighty God" or "self-sufficient God".[18]

'Femininity' has a very specific meaning here, not at all the meaning contemporary culture associates with it -- seductive, sexy, pleasure oriented, attractive to males, etc. It has the meaning of "that which supports and sustains existence", or "that which gives the power of being", or "ground of being". It has in this aspect to do with relations primarily to children, not to men. In the context of a personal God creating persons for His family, that means that the feminine side of God is

---

18 See *A Hebrew and English Lexicon of the Old Testament*, Brown, Driver, and Briggs, Oxford U. P., 1957, p. 994.

essentially a mothering image. The mothering side of God is that which supports and sustains personal life, personal being. That is exactly the meaning attached by the nursing infant to the breast, the source of nurturing and sustaining power, hence "El Shaddai".

That this was for the Hebrews a symbol also of being "almighty" and "self-sustaining" means that God was the "self-nurturing" or "self-sufficient" one. He is the one in need of nothing outside of Himself to be Himself. God can therefore be the One by whom all else receives its sustaining power of life.

The primary purpose for the man and the woman then was to reflect the image of God, to be a sacrament, an outward and visible, tangible, audible, smellable sign of the presence of God on earth. The primary purpose was not either to raise children or to be comforting to one another or sexually attractive or for the welfare of society. These are secondary aspects which follow from and are governed by the first. God was preparing to invest His very image and presence into His creation. And the man and the woman had very special and particular roles to play in that investiture.

This has a striking consequence for sexual morality. It implies that *it is not fundamental to our human nature to be **sexually** active*, that is, we can get along quite well without it as that is only one of many ways in which the prior fact of gender is sacramentally manifested.[19] It also implies that *it is fundamental to be **gender**-active*, that is manifesting the particular gift of our gender, which we shall explore below. We are to major in the gender to which we are assigned, although we may also have a well developed minor in our contra-gender characteristics. The contemporary insistence that we must be sexually active to be human comes out of materialist assumptions about our sexual nature, such as the Freudian belief that the primary dynamism of human life is the libido which is a physical, biological urge.[20]

---

19 On our alleged need to be sexually active, see below, section G, "Objective Human Nature", on two contemporary critiques of Freudian "drive" theory.

20 See remarks on Freudian libido and sublimation below, *Science - the Poisoned Well*, section entitled, "The Well and the Poison".

The story moves on into the Garden. It seems that Adam, the male of the species was created first. And so we read in 2:18 that "it is not good that the man should be alone; I will make a helper fit for him." We usually suppose that the reason it was not good for the man to be alone was that he would be lonely, he needed companionship. And that might be part of what the Lord had in mind. However, Adam was here, not merely to be comfortable and content, but with a mission, to reflect and body forth the very image of God, not only spiritually and psychologically, but physically. The physical genital organs of the man and the woman would be sacramental symbols and representations of the image of God. And being the male of the species, he could be a sacrament of only a part of that image. He needed a counterpart to assist him in that task, one who would physically, including genitally, represent the mothering side of God.

The Hebrew word for 'father' is AB, as in Abraham, "father of a multitude", or abba, "daddy". The root meaning of AB in Hebrew is "he who decides".[21]   God, of course, is the ultimate Decider, and in that sense the ultimate Father. And above all else that which He decides is the purpose for existence of all that He has created. From that decision all moral decisions flow, and in terms of that all righteous obedience is measured. God, the Author, is the source of all author-ity, for He is the source of our purpose for existence. To have authority, then, to have the freedom to do that for which I exist, means to receive from my Creator my purpose for existence.

Clearly to have authority one must be under authority. The only authority that exists anywhere in the universe is the authority of being in my purpose for existence. I come to participate in my purpose for existence by my obedience to God and by saying "yes" to His vision for my life.

While one can make more than is legitimate of word studies, the indication both from the meaning of 'AB' and from traditional Hebrew culture is that the father was the authority figure in the family, and that this was of the essence of being father,

---

21 See Herbert Bronstein, "Yahweh as Father in Hebrew Scripture", *Criterion*, Autumn-Winter, 1968-9, a publication of the Divinity School of the University of Chicago. Also Brown, Driver, and Briggs, *A Hebrew and English Lexicon of the Old Testament*, p. 3. Oxford, London, 1957.

i.e. being masculine. God, the Father of creation,
is He Who Decides. Spiritual authority must contain this element of responsible decision making or
it is no authority at all, and that is the root of
masculinity or fatherhood. The authority of earth-
ly fathers comes from they themselves being under
the authority of God, so that their authority is
not the worldy sort of authority, the ability to
"have their way". Rather, it is a responsibility
to ensure that God is getting His way.

It would seem that God, like the framers of the
American Constitution, knew that a division of powers would be to the advantage of this new arrangement He was creating. If to Adam He was giving the
gift and burden of bearing the masculine image, to
be the leader, protector, and provider, He was also
giving to Adam's mate another gift of equal weight
and importance. The two would then have to work
together to get along. Neither would ever be able
really to run rough shod over the other, for the
other would always have a built-in gift that the
other needed.

Throughout history, the archetypal image of
mother has been that which surrounds and sustains
us, originally the womb, and then the arms, lap,
and breast. To the small infant, mother is quite
literally the one "in whom I live and move and have
my being". Mother is our first and original dependency relation, the source of existence and nurturing and well being. From the pre-born infant's
point of view, mother is God and the cosmos all
wrapped up in one, the totality of existence.
Mother is she who surrounds and aids and sustains
me.

When God created Eve, He was creating one who
would surround and aid, one who would convey to me
the ability to be myself. All of the activity of
early mothering is aimed at just that, providing
the total security of sustenance such that the infant can develop a secure sense of being, an open
faith relationship to reality around him. The gift
of mothering is the gift of power.

But power is understood in the world as muscle,
money, intelligence, and the like. Power is the
ability to control circumstances to your own will.
Power from God's point of view is something quite
different, and far more fundamental and determinative. It is the power of being, the simple security and ability to be myself. Mother gives me my

first introduction to my "ground of being", my first experience of the gift of grace. It is on that foundation that all else in my life must be built. If that foundation of grace is insecure, then the whole rest of my life will be insecure.

It is this element that Adam, the male, lacked by comparison. He was not physically built to convey that kind of power in the same unique manner that Eve would be. God had to make someone who would surround and aid, and in that sense be a fit partner for Adam, who was the direction providing person.

So God divided the two gifts which were the two fundamental aspects of His own nature, the gifts of authority and of power, and thereby made the man and the woman in His image, male and female. It is only as men and women realise their gifts and are willing to share them freely and graciously and unconditionally that either family or society can flourish. That is, we must each manifest our gifts for the wholeness and welfare of those around us. Whenever we do not do that, chaos and death begin to set in. Our gifts become tools and pawns in the inevitable power struggle rather than blessings to one another. Men and women then undermine each other, using their power or their authority merely to "get their way".

But where man and woman are united in the sense that the masculine and feminine are united in God, then the true image of God is manifested here on earth in a manner most full and fitting. In God these two aspects have not so much as a hairline split between them. They are utterly mutually supportive and compatible. And so it is in the unity of man and woman that the fullness of the image of God is shown forth. That is the meaning of that curious verse which ends the creation story, the first picture of the Kingdom of heaven on earth -- "And the man and his wife were both naked, and were not ashamed." (Gen. 2:25.)

The stunning manner in which Scripture develops this theme in the relation between Yahweh and Israel, and then between Christ and His Church, is indicative of the fundamental and root nature of sexuality and gender for Biblical revelation. What we do with sexuality will in the most profound way affect our perception of the Gospel message and our ability to live that message.

We are given a pattern for masculine and feminine roles that are not mere culture creations. We have a pattern that is built into ultimate Reality, and which we are created to manifest. If 'masculine' is behavior appropriate to a male, and 'feminine' behavior appropriate to a female, we now can begin to discover the content to what is in fact "appropriate". Both men and women are given a clear identification with the image of God. Only as we see and live out the divine pattern for gender relations can our human sexual and gender relations stabalize and bear fruit as God intended, not only to populate the world with our children, but to populate His kingdom with His children, to be born not only of the flesh, but of the Spirit. Being a child of God has directly to do with being mothered and fathered by God, and our first introduction to that is our own human mothering and fathering.

It might, and no doubt will be, objected that this is a return to sexism in its worst form, patriarchy, submission of the females to male dominance. But I would argue that the Bible is not in fact a patriarchal book. The sense in which patriarchy is a destructive form of sex and gender relations is indicated by Jesus' words concerning power and authority, "lording it over" one another, using one's authority to elevate oneself over others (Mt. 20:20 ff.). Yet Jesus had no compunction about using authority: "You call me Teacher and Lord; and you are right, for so I am." (John 13:13.) This He says while washing their feet. Jesus did not abrogate authority as such, but He did radically redefine what it meant. It is clear from start to finish in Scripture that human fatherhood and authority is deeply and tragically fallen, and that the only legitimate fatherhood comes from the Father in heaven, and as a reflection of that servant image. Masculinity that does not include spiritual authority will oscillate between Rambo and a drone, super-man and a kept man. For it is only spiritual authority in the man which can stand as an equal along side of the power-of-being inherent in the woman.

It might equally be argued that this pattern would be agreeing to the worst excesses of matriarchy. To put that kind of power into the hands of women would for men be the most foolish of all possible choices, for it would give women the ability to pull the rug right out from under male identity and authority. Ironically, that of course is exactly what fallen men in a fallen world are consistently experiencing. The woman's gift of power, once one knows what to look for, is as easily recognised as the man's gift of authority. Men are deeply in fear of the feminine image, and hold it in admiration and awe and respect. That is precisely *why* they struggle so to control it. Every man knows the power of the women in his life. Is it not ridiculous to see a 250 pound linebacker type wrapped around the little finger of his 98 pound sweetheart? The power of the feminine image, the power of being, is the unrecognised (and perverted) power behind pornography and many of the other manipulative gimmicks of advertising and the media.

Patriarchy and matriarchy in the bad senses of those words are any gender roles which override and destroy the uniqueness of the other side. We therefore need to know the identity of masculinity and femininity in order to know what matriarchy or patriarchy might be. We need to know the legitimate expressions in order to spot the illegitimate expressions. And in order to know the legitimate expressions, we need to know God, whose image they reflect.

The feminist movement, which has been the home of much of our unisex philosophy and practice, has arisen partly because our culture had become in some respects hyper masculine, and has served to call our attention to many aspects of life which we had either deliberately or unwittingly ignored. And for that one must be grateful. But it must also be said that the movement itself is an anomaly as symbolized by its very title, 'feminism'. 'Feminism' is a word which, in my experience at least, most femininists (indeed, most people) have trouble giving any clear meaning.

One would suppose that a feminist movement would be dedicated to preserving feminine values. But that clearly is not the case if the traditional meaning of 'feminine' is used, so much of which feminism roundly rejects, with no other meaning forthcoming. The movement seems far more dedicated to the gaining of masculine, not feminine, values for women, a good thing if the relation between masculine and feminine are clearly understood and articulated. Much of the feminist movement appears to be more interested in gaining women the power they see men to have, a "women's power" movement, and in that sense might more accurately be called 'female-ism'. It appears to be more a movement dedicated to the female sex than to the feminine gender (as I have used 'sex' and 'gender'). But the power sought is not the power described above which I would see as the very essence of femininity. Rather it is all too often the power of the world which Jesus told His male disciples to reject, the power to control circumstances to one's own will.

Feminism has rightly called us to make sense of our masculinity and femininity and of our manhood and womanhood, and has pointed out sometimes with painful accuracy where things are amiss. But the strong tendency toward a unisex position and the inability to articulate a clear and cooperative and complementary working relation between masculinity and femininity leaves the movement still a question mark for western civilization and the Christian community.

Thomas Howard, in his extraordinary little book, *An Antique Drum*, observes:

> The human imagination, then, invests the sexual phenomenon with an importance that cannot be derived from any analysis of what seems to be occurring at the moment. Why, that is, should *this* kind of juncture of two bodies be so much more serious than *this* kind--say, shaking hands? ....
> But the view I am speaking of here--the view which suspects that the way the serious human imagination has handled the phenomenon may not be far from the truth of the matter--this view would understand the division of man into male and female as suggesting something worth considering. That is, whatever might be suggested to us by the phenomenon of man, we experience that phenomenon under two modes, male and female. The one mode has seemed to embody some such qualities as strength and courage and sovereignty, and the other gentleness and nourishment and care. And in the male and female *images*, these qualities have seemed to inhere in the hard, sinewy, hairy litheness of the one body, and in the soft, breasted fairness of the other. There appeared to be a correspondence between the *form* of the image and the nature of the being.[22]

---

22 Thomas Howard, *An Antique Drum - The World as Image*, J. B. Lippencott Co., Philadelphia and New York, p. 125.

In any event, God made the division between us after His own image. In the flesh we are mortally vulnerable to each other. No doubt that is why Jesus commands us to lay down our lives for one another (John 13). We are left with the decision to work together in our mutual vulnerability, to graciously share our gifts in our walk through life, or to live forever in the battle of the sexes. Unisex, the attempt to obliterate the warring aspects, is not the answer to the battle. Rather we must rediscover and share our gifts in our own likeness and image in God.

F. Inclusiveness and Exclusiveness

One of the primary themes of both the *Newark Report* and *Connecticut Report* is that of "inclusiveness", the characteristic of drawing into the common welfare as many and as varied persons as possible. The ultimate extreme of inclusiveness is universalism, where all are eventually saved and as a matter of principle, no one is left out. No possibility of ultimate and final damnation is allowed. At the other end of the spectrum are interpretations of salvation which arbitrarily exclude certain groups or individuals for no fault of their own, such as the exclusion of persons from heaven on the grounds that they never accepted Jesus who never had the opportunity of even hearing the Gospel.

Mainstream Christianity has resisted both of these extremes. On the one hand, the Church has maintained that our freewill really does give us the option of ultimately and eternally saying "no" to God.[23] We can look pure goodness in the face, and turn away. On the other hand, the Church has held (granted, with sometimes shaky consistency) that God does not do things that for any one of us as parents would be considered criminal or abusive. He does not command us to do something He knows we will literally be incapable of, and then find us guilty for it.

---

23 C. S. Lewis in *The Great Divorce* describes this saying of "no" to God better than anyone I know.

The theme of inclusiveness runs full current throughout most of Scripture in that all created things are meant in God's original purpose for His kingdom. In the creation story, everything is declared good. Abraham, and therefore Israel, was meant to be a blessing to all the nations of the world. "Have I any pleasure in the death of the wicked, says the Lord God, and not rather than he should turn from his way and live?" (Ezek. 18:23.)

But there is an equally powerful theme of exclusiveness. Adam and Eve are cast out of the Garden of Eden. God brings judgement on the sinful world through a flood. The Ten Commandments forbid certain activities as contrary to God's purpose and Kingdom. Jesus has clear and dire warnings both for the unrepentant and for the unforgiving.

There is a distinct tendency in contemporary liberal thinking to play down the exclusive side of God's nature, which is coupled with a near disappearance of the mascline side of the picture of God given in Scripture. God as judge, as law giver, as standing outside of the circle of creation do not appear with any consistency in the pages of either the *Newark* or *Connecticut Report*. It appears to be felt that exclusiveness is detrimental and contrary to inclusiveness, and that since we must choose between them, better to opt for the inclusive side. The choice results in the mushiness and ambiguity of thinking which we have labored to point out over these preceding pages.

The Old Testament has had a poor press in particular on the issue of inclusiveness. We are accustomed to referring to the "patriarchal" and "judgemental" God of the Old Testament in contrast to the "loving" and "inclusive" God of Jesus and the New Testament. It is not a distinction that will hold up well even granted some difficult passages (e.g., I Samuel 15). The Old Testament nevertheless was the Scripture upon which Jesus was raised, and of which He said,

Think not that I have come to abolish the law and the prophets; I have come not to abolish them but to fulfil them. For truly, I say to you, till heaven and earth pass away, not an iota, not a dot, will pass from the law until all is accomplished. (Mt. 5:17 ff.)

Jesus seemed to feel that the Law and the Prophets, i.e. the Old Testament, fairly adequately expressed what His Father wanted them to, and that rightly understood, they pointed to Himself. He considered Himself to be drawing out the natural consequences and conclusions of the Hebrew Scriptures. There is hardly a theme to be found in the New Testament anywhere that does not have its roots already deeply imbedded in the Old Testament, including emphatically that of inclusiveness.

Liberal theology today tends to pursue inclusiveness by excluding exclusiveness. Put in psychological or mythological terms, that means pursuing the feminine side of life by excluding the masculine side. Our culture and the two reports show a distinct drift toward notions that surround, sustain, and support, and away from notions that judge, analyse, uphold clear standards, or point out clear directions.

On the surface, it would appear logical to think that one became inclusive to the extent that he rejected exclusion. But the dynamic of personal and community life does not allow that. It might under one condition, namely that we were all self-sufficient beings who were not vulnerable to the activities of other beings. If that were so, it would not matter what others did or how they behaved. Our self-sufficiency would still guarantee our survival and happiness. Anyone could safely be included, no matter what his behavior. But the truth is that we are very vulnerable and very damagable by the activities and attitudes of those around us, in particular as we are growing up.

When God issued the Ten Commandments (not the Ten Suggestions), He did so for the benefit of those who were to follow them. God is self-sufficient, and does not need the commandments for His safety and welfare. But we are not, and we do. Each of the ten is a specific part of the foundation which must be in place for *any* community to survive. The ten commandments outline a framework and provide space within which a community can take place. If any one of them is omitted, the community will fail. Human nature has a structure which can be damaged and is therefore in need of "fences" to protect it from the chaos of the fallen world. The giving of the law was a major step in providing that space within which love could happen.

Love therefore *requires* exclusion of all that might violate the integrity of the community and of the persons of the community. And so, while all are indeed invited into the community, entry requires that I check my sins at the door. There is no effective forgiveness for unrepentant sin. If I value my sin more than membership in the community, then I will have my sin but not the community. If a person refuses to honor that condition, there are times when the community must take steps to exclude that person. Both Old and New Testaments are clear and unambiguous about that.

The community is the containing receptacle, that which surrounds and aids me as mother did for me in her womb. We talk of mother nature, mother church, and motherland to refer to that archetypal experience. Nature, the cosmos, is the ultimate space-time extension of that mothering power, and the family and community are the personalization of that experience. But, as we all know, that is a very fragile experience, for we can be surrounded by a desolate and hostile environment as well as a safe and nurturing one. The larger our circle of life expands, the more problematic it becomes as to whether it will be safe and nurturing or life threatening. The character of a community is to a large extent formulated by the nature of those in authority.

The Biblical revelation is founded on the experience of a Someone entering into the fallen world, the hostile, unsupportive, unnurturing space in which we hover over a pit of nothingness, Who establishes firm ground and brings order out of chaos. Love cannot happen in chaos. Somebody must take charge and establish that order. If El Shaddai, the name given to Abraham, is the mothering image of God in the Old Testament, then Yahweh, the name given to Moses leading to the giving of the law, is the masculine image, I AM, the Father who stands independently of the cosmos, the One to reckon with, in mythic terms, the Great Individual, the Great King.

The Biblical community therefore emerges with a specific structure to it, the surrounding and supporting environment personalized by specific relationships, and the head who was the "father" of the community. For the small infant, mother *is* the context, the world, the cosmos. For the older child, whose dependency relation is shifting from

101

mother to father, father is more individualized
than mother was. He is seen as not as *identical* to
that which surrounds me, but rather as the "owner"
of it, the head, the king. All the money in the
world, from the four year old's point of view,
comes out of abba's pocket.

"Belonging", then, meant being a part of the
community of which abba was the head. The slave,
the sojourner, the distant relative who came to
live in the family all understood themselves to be
"children" of the abba, the father. It was in this
context that the ethic of care for the widow, the
orphan, and the outcast carried such weight, violation of which was considered second only to idolatry in both Old and New Testaments. There was a
definitive, identifiable community to which one
might belong, a far distance from the disintegration of family life today.

We are trying today to construct "community"
through programs and social action over a base of
family disintegration. The very archtypal pattern
of community has been all but dismanteled. We try
to make things stick together, but the glue does
not hold. Community without authority is a mis-
nomer. It cannot happen.

Bishop Walmsley of Connecticut comments, if I
might take issue in the spirit of dialogue, that
there is a growing conflict between the *hierarchical* and the *organic* models for the Church, the one
in which grace flows down in a stream from the top
and the other which is a living reality indwelt by
the Spirit of God. [24]   But if we try to choose
between these two, we will end up with neither.
Organs that are alive and going anywhere have heads
that direct the limbs. Some decisions have to flow
down. We are not and cannot be an absolute democracy -- one man, one vote for every decision.

There must be a marital union between the masculine authority image and the feminine power of
being image of community life. It is out of that
marriage that spiritual children are conceived,
born, and raised into the Kingdom of God. The
whole weight of Biblical imagery of the relation
between Yahweh and Israel, and between Christ and
His Bride rests on that truth. The Marriage Feast
of the Lamb implies a union between the two

---

24 In the Connecticut diocesan newspaper, *Good News*, October 1987, p. 3.

archetypal aspects of reality, carried out in the context of this sacramental world of space and time.

Inclusiveness, then, means "belonging to" someone in particular, not just to a group in general, which is why the "realm" of God does not adequately substitute for the kingship of God.[25] That person can be another human being, a circumstance which always leads, due to our dependent nature, to idolatry. Jesus told Nicodemus that if he wanted to see the Kingdom of God, he would have to be born again, i.e., to move his dependency (childhood) from the circumstances around him (the Hebrew community and created order) to God Himself (outside the creation). It was not enough to be a son of Abraham and of the Hebrew community. He would have to be fathered by God and mothered by God. Then he could be a son of God and would see the Kingdom of God. Otherwise he would see only the kingdoms of this world, the competitive, ratrace, dog eat dog kingdoms out of which the Lord came to save us in the first place. Why else would Jesus use the sexual imagery of birth and family life, and why else would the themes of a marriage between God and the world run so consistently throughout Scripture?

When the fathering side of life is missing or lame in a community, the individuation process is hindered. One of any growing individual's primal fears is that of losing one's identity in the the mothering image, of getting swallowed up in the family or community. That is why we go through the "terrible two's" and that is why, often, we experience the ferocity of the teenage rebellion. A healthy fathering side of life always points beyond the given community to an independent source of life. Father takes this role in assisting the young child to separate from mother, the initial and primary dependency relation. Father helps the child to move from under the wing of his literal physical mother out to a wider experience of being mothered. The mothering, sustaining, nurturing circle expands. Other authority figures, especially employers, take this role in helping us to separate from family ties. Father God takes this role with us in our relation to the wider communities we inhabit and the widest circle of creation. No matter how wide our circle of life expands, it

---

25 See discussion of the *Newark Report* above, "Sexuality and Family Life -- The Biblical Roots", section II B, "Kingdom or Realm? - The Loss of Personal Focus".

can never outrun God, so we can be always rooted in a safe relation with God. We can live in the circle of creation without losing our identity to it. Our citizenship, our basic identity, really is from heaven, very much in this world, but not of it.

There is, then, a Biblical sort of inclusiveness. But it does not rely on a "pluralistic" view of life, which is really a view that has lost its confidance about getting at the truth of basic matters. If we are having trouble getting at the truth, let us say that, but let us not pretend that we can all be right even when we believe contradictory things. Biblical inclusiveness takes its stand squarely on objective truth. Anyone who wants to live in the truth (live in the light - I John 1:5 ff.) and who is willing to discipline him or herself to follow Jesus *will* find the truth. Jesus has staked His honor on it. The Bible does not allow for the inclusion of false gods or false views of life. And the Bible does not allow for the inclusion of unrepentant sinners, that is, those who will not accept being dependent on the hand of God and standing under His authority, those who will not accept being mothered and fathered by God. For only so can they become His children. God is inviting us into His family, the primary and ultimate symbol of inclusion.

Given the Hebraic notion of community, Sarah can be comfortably included in Abraham. Our rampant individualism will not accept that kind of inclusiveness and therefore wants to find the "marginalized" people included in some other way. But it may be that no other way will in fact accomplish the required inclusiveness, only a family with clear fathering and mothering images lived out and pointing on to God as our ultimate Parent.

This latter point is the primary argument, in my opinion, against the ordination of women within the Christian community. The priesthood and episcopate are above all leadership roles with therefore a heavy emphasis on the masculine side. If a healthy community requires a clear delineation of masculine and feminine roles, then a male priesthood would be in order.[26]

G. Objective Human Nature

The *Connecticut Report's* discussion of the homosexual issue is founded on a discussion of human nature (*objective* human nature, interestingly enough). Freud, or his school, appears to be their main source of information on our sexual nature:

> The teachings of Freud and the psycho-dynamic theorists who followed him have added yet another dimension to our understanding of the place of sexuality in our lives. Within this framework, sexuality or libido, as defined by Freud, is a major source of our creative energy, but in the process *drives* the organism towards a higher level of development. (p. 9. My emphasis.)

What one does not learn from the report is that only *some* of those "psycho-dynamic theorists" who followed after Freud indeed followed Freud. Alfred Adler split from Freud specifically on the issue of "drive" in favor of a more "purposive" understanding of the unconscious, as have many others. From Adler's point of view, the unconscious was goal oriented rather than "driven". Or, if we are driven, we are also in a significant way the driver.

---

26 The issue of women's ordination cannot be fully discussed here. I will have a work ready in early 1988 which will provide connections more fully between the spiritual and psychological sides of the issues, *Yahweh or the Great Mother? -- Man and Woman in the Image of God*. See endnote on Emmaus Ministries for details.

It is clear in any event that much work needs to be done in understanding and developing the nature of the feminine role and gift in the life of the Church, and in working through to a creative and mutually compatible relationship between the masculine and feminine sides of life. My belief is that that will happen spontaneously as women discover the nature of the power of being, and as men discover the true and Godly nature of spiritual authority.

Adler's psychology is in this respect far more compatible with a Christian understanding of human nature.[27]

Whether we are speaking of cosmological development of the human race or of individual psychology, we must have freedom at the beginning of the process or we will not find it at the end. If freedom is not a basic part of how the universe comes into being, there will be no way of inserting it at some point down the line. If the world was not called into being as a free act of will by a purposive creator God, then freedom will not be derived out of some deft combination of determinisms. Nor will a sprinkling of "chance" to loosen up the deterministic structure produce rational freedom. If the cosmos is essentially either determined or a result of chance, then the emergence of rational freewill will find neither explanation nor source. Similarly with individual psychology, if rational freewill is not a part of our basic given nature, then no amount of manipulation of the givens will produce or explain freedom.

Any theory of "drives", therefore, as the basic underlying dynamism of human nature will obliterate the sense in which we can be individuals of freewill, morally responsible before God or each other. If the "drive" theory is fundamentally correct, then not one of the primary doctrines of the Christian faith can be true. The Biblical doctrines of creation and of salvation both fall because moral responsibility before God is assumed in each. We cannot have it both ways. This is not to

---

27 Perhaps Adler's best known work is *Social Interest, A Challenge to Mankind*, Faber and Faber, London, 1938. An excellent introduction to his work, with extensive and well organized excerpts from his writing is *The Individual Psychology of Alfred Adler*, by Heinz and Rowena Ansbacher, Basic Books, New York, 1956.

Adler writes in *Social Interest*: "Psychology underwent a renaissance with the advent of [Freudian] psycho-analysis. This resurrected the omnipotent Ruler of human destiny in the form of sexual libido and conscientiously depicted in the unconscious the pains of hell, and original sin in the 'sense of guilt'." The success of psycho-analysis "was due to the predisposition of the immense number of pampered persons who willingly accepted the views of psycho-analysis as rules universally applicable, and who were thereby confirmed in their own [pampered] style of life." (P. 35 and 36.)

Clearly if I am "driven" into sexual expression, I cannot be found guilty of that expression. The narcissistic obsession for comfort and pleasure is found after all to be a virtue.

imply that there are no drives, but rather that any drives or unconscious mechanisms that we have must be understood in the context of rational freewill.

Quentin Hyder, a psychiatrist practicing in Darien, Connecticut, and in New York City, wrote to the *Darien News-Review*, 1/7/88, in a letter to the editor dialogue:

.... My greatest concern however is Dr. Gargiulo's denial that homosexuals have voluntary control over their actions. He states "they frequently feel a powerful compulsion, despite their best intentions, toward a given action." So what? Are homosexuals less capable of self control than heterosexuals? I also frequently felt a "powerful compulsion" toward fornication during my happy bachelor days, but I chose not to indulge for personal and moral reasons. Dr. Gargiulo may not comprehend this philosophy -- it is called celebacy. It is *not* a deprivation. In my case it was a significant factor in sustaining my healthy sense of self-esteem. It is totally fallacious to teach that men and women need to be sexually active to live a fulfilled and satisfying life. It is to the shame of my profession that I confess that most of my colleagues preach this lie, and thereby lead astray countless patients who have turned to them for guidance. Homosexuals can choose to be celebate, just as millions of heterosexuals do.

My own experience echos that of Dr. Hyder. I made it, by the grace of God, a virgin into my marriage. And the disaster around us only confirms the wisdom of that decision. If homosexuals are indeed *unable* to sustain chastity, that is *ipso facto* evidence of a pathology, not of a natural and uncontrollable drive, just as with heterosexuals. If they are *unwilling*, that is evidence of sin and perhaps an inbred pampered-child life style.

The report, however, accepts the alleged conclusions of psychology, a "scientific discipline", that the condition of homosexuality is a given inborn fact for some persons.

It is clear to us, as to scientific researchers, that there is, indeed, a spectrum of human sexual *natures* as well as *behaviors*.

What is clear to us is that *scientific research and method have concluded* that there are homosexual and heterosexual persons. (p. 19. My emphasis.)[28]

The report accepts the distinction between situational, socialized, and constitutional homosexuality, the latter being that which is inborn, the given "nature" (as distinct from behavior, which can be a choice).

...the constitutionally homosexual person has no choice about his or her sexual orientation. The task of the constitutionally homosexual person is to integrate the sexual part of his/her psyche into the whole person, rather than to ignore it or repress it. The goal of such development is a person whose self concept and behavior is an expression of his or her true nature. (p. 20.)[29]

It is expected, therefore, that such persons will seek and live out homosexual unions. The report does say that promiscuous unions are not acceptable, but that unions representing loyalty and faithfulness are within the bounds of acceptable Christian behavior. Regarding Biblical passages admittedly forbidding same-sex unions, the report says that this refers to situational or social homosexuality by persons who are by nature really heterosexual. Since they are violating their "nature", their behavior therefore is rightly condemned (one presumes) by Paul and *Leviticus*. Significantly, these sorts of homosexual behaviors are also still considered pathological and therefore candidates for medical intervention even according to the A. P. A. decision which removed homosexuality from its diagnostic listings.[30]

There is a wide spectrum of sexual orientations and behaviors, and each of us is called to act in accordance with our particular "natures" or orientation, whether homosexual or heterosexual. In all cases we are called from Creation to use the gift of our sexuality responsibly and, being a redeemed people, as a way of connecting ourselves more closely to the Divine Lover.

---

28 See the following article, "Science -- the Poisoned Well", for an assessment of the "pansexual" view of human nature which these quotations evidence.

29 See below, section J, "Inclusiveness in the Dialogue", for Dr. Hyder's comments on the "constitutionality" of the homosexual nature and the A.P.A. decision to remove homosexuality from its diagnostic listings.

30 Ibid.

> The conflict of opinions about sexual minorities
> often centers around their choice to act from their
> sexual nature.... Such a separation of action from
> nature is unbiblical and inconsistent with a theolo-
> gy which has as its core the unity of God's nature
> and action. (p. 21.)

Consider the moral confusion opened up by such a
view. How do I know for sure which is my nature?
If I occasionally want a same-sex union, how do I
know whether I am bi-sexual or a heterosexual violating my "nature"? Can bestiality be my "nature"?
Or incest? Or rape? The *only one* of these behaviors not yet publicly defended in print is forcible
rape. And that has to be included also if one
counts the mindless suggestiveness of pornography.

The case for acceptance of homosexual behavior
rests completely on the prior acceptance of the
homosexual "nature" as a given, over which he has
no choice. And this conclusion is attributed to
"scientific research and method" (see quote above).
But neither scientific research nor method ever
concluded a thing in their whole lives. Scientific
researchers and methodologists did all the conclud-
ing, always in the context of their larger philosophical and theological commitments (or non-com-
mitments).

Even a quick look through the field would seem
to make two points clear, even for a non-expert.
First, it is simply not true that the scientific
evidence is really that clearly decided upon within
the scientific community. And secondly, even if it
were, there would still be issues to be met.

*   *   *   *

To establish the first point, the following
rather extensive quote from a currently used college textbook gives some indication of the lack of
unity on the issues we are discussing among the
scientific community. In the preface to *Understanding Development*, the authors note:

> Developmental psychology is changing. Many books
> are still rooted in ideas that have been discarded
> in the mid 1980's.[31]

---

31 *Understanding Development*, by Sandra Scarr, Richard A. Weinberg, and Ann Levine.
   Harcourt, Brace, Jovanovich, 1986, p. iii.

Whatever happened to stabile, monolithic science?
This might be advertizing hype to sell the "latest
stuff", but anyone familiar with the current scene
in psychology knows there is truth to this claim.
Chapter 13, "Let's Get Physical: Growth, Puberty,
and Sexuality", contains an examination of the
Freudian position on which both the *Newark* and the
Connecticut Report rely. The authors are critical
of the Freudian position, as many have been ever
since he first published his ideas, precisely along
those lines that would be of interest to the issues
of this article, namely Freud's sense of sexuality
as a biological given, and of the libido as an
innate sex urge which *drives* to find expression.
In a section entitled, "Cultural Scripts", relating
how different cultures deal with sexuality, we
read:

> In Australia, Aranda couples make love, sleep, make
> love again, four or five times a night, every night.
> Couples in the Irish folk community on the island of
> Inis Beag consider having sexual intercourse once or
> twice a month more than enough. Husbands and wives
> never fully undress in front of one another. The
> men feel that sex is debilitating; the women do not
> experience orgasms. They are one of the only groups
> anthropologists have studied that does not have a
> 'dirty joke' tradition.
>
> The Dani of West New Guinea...are a special case:
> They are not interested in sex. Like many other
> pre-industrial peoples who lack modern birth con-
> trol, the Dani observe a postpartum taboo. A hus-
> band and wife do not engage in sexual intercourse
> for some time after the birth of the child. In most
> such societies abstinence lasts one or two years; in
> Dani society it lasts four to six years. As far as
> Heider could tell, the taboo was never violated.
> Are the Dani seething with frustration? No. Do
> they believe there is a terrible punishment for
> breaking the taboo? No. When pressed, they say
> that their ancestors might be annoyed, but the Dani
> do not take ancestral ghosts very seriously. Do
> husbands or wives engage in other forms of sexual
> activity (masturbation or homosexual relations) dur-
> ing the long period of marital abstinence? Again,
> the answer is no. Heider's questions baffled them:
> what is so important about sex?

To be sure, the Dani are only one small society. But they and other groups who adapt easily to celibacy (priests and nuns, for example) raise questions about a central theme in Freud's theory. Freud saw sexuality as the expression of a powerful innate drive that, like hunger and thirst, demands fulfillment. From this point of view, the development of sexual interests and activities in adolescence is biological in origin. Hormones cause a boy to lust after a girl in the second row of his French class and prevent a girl who is wondering when her date will make his move from concentrating on a play.

John Gagnon and William Simon (1973) question the entire notion of a sex drive and the power of homones to control social behavior. Yes, many Western adolescents seek sexual relations; but how much of their behavior is due to hormones, and how much is due to social expectations? Parents and peers are watching and waiting. Dating, going steady, falling in love, and lust are part of the script that Western culture writes for adolescents. In pursuing the opposite sex, young people may be performing their social roles, not just obeying their gonads. Adolescents may engage in sexual activity to prove their maturity, establish their independence, win peer approval, confirm their gender identity, or perhaps to rebel against adult authority and social conventions....

In short, physiological maturation makes sex possible. Early sensual and affectionate experiences make it probable. But cultural scripts largely determine the who, what, when, where, and why of sexuality.[32]

It would appear that the appeal to "science" and to "scientific method" of either the *Newark* or the *Connecticut Report* has missed the mark. There is clear empirical evidence weighing heavily against a notion of a "nature", to which we are bound and which, Biblically or otherwise, we are called to express in the manner suggested. One had best not go about quoting "science" as though that were an entity to whom one could go and ask, "Did you really say that?" -- unless of course one knows a fellow by the name of "Science". We would do better

---

32 Ibid., p. 513 ff. Also see below, similar comments by Dr. W. R. Coulson.

to quote specific scientists, and then examine whether they had adequate reason for saying it. That, after all, is the scientific way.

It may well be that given a particular programming by early childhood or adolescent experience, that it would be very difficult for one to get out of a particular behavior pattern, such as homosexuality. But the assertion that it is built in and not at all a matter of choice needs to be assessed for its reliability.

The desire for reasonable discussion and dialogue on the issue of constitutional homosexuality is beset by the ominous and darkening shadow of AIDS. The Christian community will surely be tested to the limits of endurance and beyond, to trust and walk in the grace of God in its relation to those afflicted, in particular the gay community.

On one hand, many responsible Americans are responding with the only rational and compassionate advice possible under the circumstance. Surgeon General Koop, Education Secretary Bennett, Health and Human Services Secretary Bowen, and President Reagen have all called for mutually faithful monogamous relationships. And on the other hand, the majority of the gay community appears adamantly set in its defense of the homosexual life-style, including the pursuit of a free-wheeling sex life, based on the assertion that we human beings cannot reasonably be expected to renounce our sexual freedom, that the unbounded expression of sexual urges is a necessity for the full experience of our humanness.

W. R. Coulson, Ph. D., clinical psychologist at the United States International University in San Diego, helps to take the heat off of the sexual issue in his observation that:

> Normal people are neither heterosexual nor homosexual, and certainly not bisexual: normal people are not occupied with sex. If there is one nearly universal occupation of Americans, it is their families....

> My wife and I have children, so I must be a heterosexual; but I don't *define* myself that way. People don't *define* themselves by their sexuality -- except homosexuals do....

Dr. Coulson takes the interesting tack of putting teens in the role of parents where he finds them exhibiting considerably greater sense of moral responsibility and interest in rational discussion of the moral issues.

Children are capable of exceptional clarity of moral vision, especially *when invited to consider the requirements of a better life for their children.*[33] [Fox emphasis.]

In effect he does an end run around the teenage sense of immortality and invulnerability by asking them about their own potential children. They apparently do not see their potential teen children as the superteens they imagine themselves to be, at least in the face of their own parents. Moral uprightness does not seem so impossible for their children-to-be as it seemed at first for themselves.

According to Dr. Coulson, Dr. Marc Conant, "the foremost AIDS expert in San Francisco",[34] in a radio interview in November of 1985 said that the gay community in San Francisco was increasing in its percentage of AIDS infection at the rate of 10% per year. By the end of 1985, 50% were carrying the AIDS virus. Homosexual men, although "safe sex" is the talk of the gay community, are unable to control the spread of AIDS. The present rate of infection is in excess of 70%.[35] Coulson said in a talk to a group of students:

We're going to see the end of the gay community, not only in San Francisco but in the whole country within our lifetime -- because of those hundreds and thousands of anonymous sexual partners which are part of the gay lifestyle....

It's called genocide. It's the obliteration of an entire race, of people. If you can think of gay men in San Francisco as a race, there won't be any more gay men; because they cannot learn that lesson. They keep having sex. *Because they define themselves by their sexuality.*[36] [Fox emphasis.]

---

33 W. R. Coulson, *How to Talk to Kids about Homosexuality*, available from Nevermore Assoc., Box 8337, La Jolla, CA 92038. Tel. 619-560-0361

34 Op. cit., p. 4.

35 Ibid., p. 3.

36 Ibid., p. 3, 5.

113

Or, more accurately, they define themselves by their sexual activity. If gender, not sex, is the ontological reality of "who we are", if gender is prior to sex as a reflection of our image in God, then we can indeed partially define our nature by our gender. But the horrendous consequences of defining ourselves by a specific activity of gender, namely sex, is becoming all too apparent. We may find ourselves locked into into behavior that can only be described as suicidal.

The ploy of diverting criticism of homosexual behavior by saying that that is an attack on their identity or innate nature has backfired in the most devastating way.[37]

To put to final rest the assertion that we are "driven" by our sexual urges, Dr. Coulson said to his students:

> And it frightens me to think that our AIDS education in the state of California is going to be shaped by a homosexualist orientation; because we'll be told that "While it would be nice if you can be abstinent, who can expect it? It's too hard to be abstinent."
> Well, don't believe it.... And let me offer you, in proof of that proposition, the Chinese experience.
> There are one billion, 50 million people in mainland China.... Ninety-nine percent of them -- this is what the Chinese vice-consul in San Francisco told me two days ago -- "Ninety-nine percent of them," he said, "follow the old lules." He said, "The old lules include 'abstinence before marriage'". I said, "What's the average age of marriage in China?" And he said, "Among the young people in the countryside, they tend to get married in their late teens or early twenties, because they need to get married and work the farms." Most people in China live in agricultural areas and they work as farmers. But he said, "In the cities, particularly among the intellectuals, marriage is delayed until the mid-twenties, the late-twenties." He said, "Intellectuals often don't get married until their mid-thirties." I said, "And you mean to say they don't have sex until their mid-thirties?" And he said, "Sure!" And he said it again: "Sure!" I was taking notes, and I put in exclamation points,

---

37 See below, *Science - the Poisoned Well*, at the end of section entitled, "The Babylonian Captivity of Science", on the "victim" strategy of the gay rights movement.

because this is what it sounded like: "Sure!
Sure!" He added, "That's the principle!"
   I said, "Don't they suffer from this?"
   He said, "Not that I know of."
   In other words, if you are expected to be sexually active and you are *not* sexually active, you will
tend to think of yourself as being in pain.... But
if you know, first, that the smart people are not
sexually active and, two, that *nobody* should be sexually active until they're in a mutually monogamous,
one-time, lifetime marriage, you're not going to
feel bad about not being sexually active....

Dr. Coulson added the following footnote:

Doc Nevermore [the imaginary doctor whom Dr. Coulson
was impersonating as he talked with his group of
students] meant "the old rules" but got carried away
with Chinese locution. (Having interviewed Chinese
medical students who were studying in the U. S. and
having come to understand from them that premarital
abstinence was normative and common in China -- no
less in the present generation than in the long ago
-- he had called the consulate to check an offical
source. Emphatically did the vice-consul confirm
this understanding, as several additional sources
have since.)

*   *   *   *

   The second point I wish to make is that even if
there should be cases of constitutional homosexual
or bi-sexual nature, it still remains to be answered whether that is "normal" in the sense that
it is right and good. There are people, apparently, who are born schizophrenic, there are people
born with low intelligence, and a host of other
conditions, of which no one but an insurance company would say, this is "an act of God", even though
they have no choice in the matter. Is a condition
God-given simply because one has no or limited
choice in the matter? Are compulsive gamblers or
alcoholics simply working out their "nature"? And
if homosexuality and bi-sexuality are biological or
genetic givens, are these conditions then candidates for genetic engineering to work on? The implications before us are earth shaking.

   How do we distinguish between those givens which
are given by God and those which are in some sense
which we may not understand, given by the fallen-
ness of the spiritual, social, moral, political,
cultural, biological, and physical world around us?

It is simply impossible to make that determination apart from knowing the will of God, not only practically impossible, but logically impossible. Clearly we are in need of some objective standard of what is "normal". But that is precisely what science and scientific method *per se* cannot give us. That is something which can come *only* from an authority higher than ourselves, for only that can rescue the matter out of cultural and moral relativism and the resulting morass of confusion, manipulation, and power struggle which always fills the moral vacuum.

H. The Stakes:
Revelation, Natural Theology, and Natural Science

The Biblical doctrine of creation, that God created the cosmos and that therefore the cosmos itself is stamped with His nature, implies that the scientific empirical method which investigates that world that God created, will reveal something to us of Himself. If that is so, then Christians can only rejoice at the development of scientific method and in its appropriate use in religious matters. The very fact of creation implies science and the scientific method. Natural theology, the attempt to understand the nature of God through reason and through observation of the world around us, and natural science, the investigation of the world, are both a consequence of Genesis 1:1.

The other, and religiously more common understanding of our knowledge of God, is revelation. God tells us something rather than we figuring something out through experience and reason independently of God speaking to us. This is usually associated with Scripture as the receptacle of accumulated revelation from God, but also with God speaking to us individually about our lives, which is the way the receptacle got filled in the first place.

Reason and revelation are not opposites that we must choose between them. Revelation is a personal experience about which we then reason. The purpose for our minds is to relate to the reasonableness of God. God relates to us reasonably, something we can experience only by being drawn out of our positions of brokenness, pain, darkness, ignorance, arrogance, and willfullness, that is to say, by discipleship and the cross life.

With the onslaught of secular humanism and the rise of secular science came also the downfall of natural theology. Since the late middle ages, it had been increasingly thought, other than in Catholic circles for the most part, that it was not possible to reason from the existence of the world to knowledge of God, and that we therefore had to make do with revelation alone as a source of knowledge about God or His will for us. Revelation seemed to be pushed further and further into a defensive corner, the Roman Church finally drawing the line beyond which it would not retreat with the decision to believe that the Pope was, on certain matters, infallible. The Evangelical wing of Christendom matched that move with its similar doctrine of the infalliblity of the Bible.

These moves were made because the arena of truth testing, which had been the studies of the philosophers and theologians, was moved out into the public arena of empirical testing and made available in principle to anybody who cared to examine the issues. It did not seem, from that place, that evidence for God fared very well. And it seemed that the world did alright quite by itself, thank you.

When the Church lost the battle for natural theology, it also lost the integrity of the doctrine of creation and its believability in the face of secularism. There was no longer any common ground upon which the Christian could intellectually challenge the world around him, for Christians, or most of them, were giving up the exploration and understanding of the world to the secular people, which left only the material and authority of revelation as a means of communicating the Gospel. Having lost the first major battle, most Christians did not feel we could risk Scripture and revelation to a similar fate, hence the doctrines of infallibility.

The fullness of the Biblical understanding of creation implies that God is revealing Himself both through creation and through speaking to us. It implies that the world is good to investigate, but that the world is not self-explanitory and therefore needs an interpreting word, all of which has been abundantly verified by secularism's bankrupt

117

attempt to found the world on itself. We can find out certain things by empirical investigation, such as what a thing is capable of under given circumstances. But knowing what it is capable of, which might be a whole range of items, does not tell us what it is *for*, which might be only one or a few of the capability list. To find out why a thing exists, what it is for, you have to ask the one responsible for its existence. Empirical investigation is impotent to tell us that. What a thing is for, the reason for existence, is the basis for the moral dimension of life. And that of logical necessity requires revelation. You just have to be told.

The implications of this for our previous discussion on human nature and sexuality are obvious. We need to listen to God to find out what He has in mind for our sexual nature. Empirical investigation might help us define the limits of our sexual potential, but it cannot define for us the purpose of it nor what the ideal or healthy form of it is. Thus when the Christian community loses the integrity of its theology such that natural theology cannot compliment and back up revelation, then the integrity of our witness to the world is compromised, with the consequences we can see of the last three centuries. The people who are looking at the world are not listening to the people who are listening to God, and usually vice versa. Christians have tried to listen to the voice of God from above, and to step out in obedience, but so often with the queasy feeling of the ground beneath dropping out from under us.

But the last three centuries have also led to the disintegration of the secular ability to answer the deep questions of life. On one occasion at my stay at Oxford, I was part of a small group of students sitting in the room of a well known philosopher. For one reason or another I raised the question, "If things do not have to exist as they are, why then does anything exist at all?" -- *the* question of natural theology. To which the famous philosopher replied, "We don't ask that question anymore." I felt as though I had said something in bad taste, and it was not till ten minutes after leaving the session that I realized, "What do you mean, <u>we</u> don't ask that anymore?! *I just asked it*!" What he meant was, "I do not know why things exist if they do not have to."

Secular materialism is bankrupt of ultimate pre-suppositions. And it does not know what to make of its need for them. Since the technological end of the world continues to work anyhow without the secular scientist's knowledge of them, he continues on his way, thinking of himself as a success. By the grace of You-Know-Who, the rain continues to fall on the just and the unjust, natural law continues to function.

Re-enter natural theology, which is all about those ultimate presuppositions. Revelation, natural theology, and natural science must stand together, another three-legged stool. Neither one nor two can stand alone, or at best lamely. Reality is too intricately interdependent for us to separate out or ignore any fundamental aspect without impairing the others as well.

I.   The Meeting Place

This is not the place to re-establish natural theology.[38] But a few things can be said about our ability to take on the world in the intellectual arena. If all truth is from God, then we have nothing to fear from science. It is unquestionably one of the most brightly shining gifts from God to His fallen world, and can serve only to bring us closer to Him, properly used.

But "properly used" requires knowing the *purpose* of it, which means we must ask its Creator why we have it. And that means revelation, listening to God, and to those others who listen and who have listened to God. Unless one reduces science to the barest and most sterile technology, one *cannot* be a good scientist without an active prayer life. Without prayer we can be good technicians, but not, in the full sense, good scientists.

If science involves listening to God, then it is also going to be a realm in which spiritual warfare takes place. It is the intent of God that science be used for His purposes and no other. Many will take that to be an intrusion of authoritarian religious bias into the place of honest inquiry, and

---

38 My efforts in that direction are contained in *Personality, Empiricism, and God*, to be available early in 1988. See endnote on Emmaus Ministries for further details and other items.

the death knell of science. Just who is sounding which death knell for science we will look into more deeply in the following article. But suffice it to say that whether or not religious institutions behave themselves in this matter any more than secular institutions (as per Communist Russia or Nazi Germany), it still remains that the secular world has not been able to explain the ontological basis for why science operates whereas the Biblical worldview can do exactly that.[39]

God will make His claim on scientific activity. That is not to say that God means to stack the deck in His favor such that honest inquiry will be thwarted. God requires our belief in Him, but *only* on the basis of an open and honest search for truth. God named Himself "I AM" to Moses at the burning bush, the "God-who-is", not the "God-who-isn't". He is the God who can be found if we seek Him with all our heart, mind, and strength. Seeking God does not mean leaping in the dark, but looking around with a teachable spirit, a heart that is open to reality, including spiritual reality, and asking honest questions.

With God's permission, then, or rather His insistence, we have one commitment prior to our commitment to Him, and that is our commitment to the truth, whatever it is. God is willing to rest His case on His own reality and on His own ability to reveal Himself to us -- if we have teachable spirits, that is, if we really are interested in the truth, at any cost.

That means that the *fundamental activity of spiritual warfare is not casting out demons, but staying open to the truth and insistently maintaining an arena of openness within which others can have a dialogue with oneself.* Demons tend not to stick around where the light of truth is shining. And that means that we can expect that the fundamental activity of the anti-Christ will be to obfuscate efforts to maintain that openness to the truth. Jesus is not being merely picturesque when He describes Satan:

---

39 See my book, *Personality, Empiricism, and God*, to be available in the fall of 1988, offering the philosophical justification for saying that empirical science logically presupposes the existence of the Biblical sort of God.

Jesus said to them, "If God were your Father, you
would love me, for I proceeded and came forth from
God; I came not of my own accord, but He sent me.
Why do you not understand what I say. It is because
you cannot bear to hear my word. You are of your
father the devil, and your will is to do your father's desires. He was a murderer from the beginning, and has nothing to do with the truth, because
there is no truth in him. When he lies, he speaks
according to his own nature, for he is a liar and
the father of lies." (John 8:42 ff.)

The efforts of the philosophic or scientific
community to clarify methods for getting at the
truth and to provide a communal arena in which the
truth can be shared and investigated is emminently
from God. Christians ought to be in the front
ranks of such endeavors, not quaking in fear lest
our favorite doctrine be disproven. If it be disproven, we are better off without it. If, as Jesus
said, in following His commandments we become truly
His disciples, and in doing so know the truth that
will set us free, then being a disciple of Jesus
must be the world's best course in truth finding
and truth living.[40] Maintaining that kind of
truth-seeking is the first priority of all spiritual warfare -- from God's point of view. It can
only be one of the Enemy's ploys to divide the
Christian community from honest inquiry because it
strikes right at the heart of our trust in God as a
God of truth.

And that indeed was one of the effects of the
fall from grace in Genesis 3, the figs leaves being
the symbols of the psychological and spiritual
closed circle of self-sufficient defensiveness.
Having taken leave of God, we retreated into a
fortress mentality in which truth becomes the lack-
ey of an obessesive drive for security and comfort.

Christians are given only one offensive weapon
in their spiritual armor, the sword of the Spirit,
which is the word of God (Ephesians 6:17). If God
is the "God who is", and if the God who is speaks
"what is", not "what isn't", then our efforts to
understand what is in the world, honestly and
humbly pursued, can only be a part of our faith,
not a contradiction to it.

---

40 John 8:31 ff.

The Biblical community has at times suffered persecution in the world, sometimes because we deserved it. We suffered for our sins, not for our faith. The sword of the Spirit is a two edged sword, we are to speak the truth, but in love. There are times when we speak the truth, but not in love, and there are times when we are trying to be loving, but fail in speaking the truth.

But there are times when the Biblical community suffers for its witness to truth as it truly understands it from God. This persecution consistently has arisen when the Biblical community refused to be submerged into the paganism around them and steadfastly maintained their unique message of the sovereignty and salvation of God. The perennial philosophy and way of life will in one form or another be at the root of such persecution.

If Christians, then, are going to be a witness to the world about the God who created the world, we will have to get methods for truth seeking and truth testing under our belts, and we will have to be better at it than anyone else. Science *is* those methods, common sense honed to a fine edge, in a manner appropriate to the material at issue. It is asking the question, "How do you know?" to any statement of fact, in a logical and systematic and probing way. We will have to learn to think logically and consistently, and to expect of ourselves and others clear answers insofar as we can obtain them, sometimes having to make do with less than the ideal, but moving ahead wherever we can.

The secular people did not win the battle over natural theology, we gave it to them. We did not take seriously that our God is a God of truth, and that therefore all legitimate truth-seeking methods will sooner or later lead to Him. We have on the whole not been willing to risk our faith in the arena of truth testing. We were out gunned, we thought. And so we hid behind the impenetrable shield of infallibility, and the sword of the Spirit stayed sheathed in its scabbard.

If we are serious about meeting the intellectual challenge of the world around us, we will have to put down the shield of infallibility and take up again the shield of faith, the trust that truth really is of God, and that in the chaos of the world, as we listen to and obey our God, He will lead us into truth that will indeed answer our questions and resolve our dilemmas. That will not

122

give us "easy" answers, but it will give us good and reliable answers. We will lose some battles because we are in this world sometimes in truth outgunned. But we are not outgunned in truth, and so the war is already won.

One does not want to raise intellectual debate over other aspects of the spiritual life, the intuitive or volitional. The heart often has reasons of which the mind knows little, which are very much in touch with reality. We each need to resolve that balance within ourselves and to keep open to the various channels of truth we experience without letting one channel run rough shod over the others.

In that light, the doctrines of infallibility are not necessarily heavy handed authoritarianism crushing freedom of inquiry. Rather, given the historical context of increasing hyper-intellectualization of western culture, the assertion of infallibility was in part a cry of "enough!" from the intuitive side of ourselves which knew that something was deeply amiss but was not yet able to articulate what it was in intellectually acceptable ways. Dostoyevsky put the matter very well in *Notes from the Underground,* a short story about a person in rebellion against the way logic and reason seemed to be crushing the free spirit of man in the emerging industrial culture.

> "Good Lord," they'll scream at you, "you can't possibly deny that: twice two *is* four! Never does nature ask you for your opinion; she does not care a damn for your wishes, or whether you like her laws or not...." But, goodness gracious me, what do I care for the laws of nature and arithmetic if for some reason or other I don't like those laws of twice-two?[41]

The tide has turned, however, and the intellectual picture is, I believe, emerging in stunning fashion on the side of reason *and* freedom, the material creation *and* our spiritual roots, being complements, not opposites. So we can thank God for those who out of personal integrity either stood their ground, or honestly searched through new approaches. Only God Himself can put it all together.

---

41 From *The Best Short Stories of Dostoyevsky,* trans. by David Magarshack, Modern Library, Random House, New York. P. 118.

Most Christians do not live on this heady philosophical plane. For most of us the level of engagement with the world is the pastoral and moral
issues of daily life. Both the *Newark* and *Connecticut Report* rightly urge us to listen to those
with whom we disagree on these levels. There must
be a place of meeting, no matter how deeply we
disagree with our opposite. There must be a place
where those (Christian or otherwise) who defend the
homosexual position or the bi-sexual position, or
any other imaginable position, can sit with Christians and share their beliefs and commitments and
feelings.

But every meeting place must have basic ground
rules, and it is those ground rules which are established at the philosophical level. That is,
there must be agreement about there being an objective truth at all. That is a basic part of the
common ground between any two persons, that there
is a common world which we inhabit about which we
can learn and share. There must be agreement on
the rules of truth-seeking and truth-testing, which
are none other than the common rules of logic and
of scientific investigation appropriate to a given
area.

The meeting place must be an arena in which any
suggestion can be entertained, no matter how absurd, and also an arena in which any suggestion can
be fairly criticized for its worth. No one leg of
the stool of faith can override the other, each
must do its part in concert with the others like a
dance.

These are the intellectual rules. But there are
also spiritual rules necessary to follow for the
success of truth seeking, by far the more difficult
to put in place. These rules recognise the fact
that the arena of truth seeking is not populated by
ideas but by very vulnerable persons who are risking something to share their ideas. Thus the arena
must have an atmosphere such that one is *encouraged*
to share those ideas he has, no matter how absurd
he feels they may be in the eyes of others, and
encouraged to examine and assess ideas, no matter
how much risk of conflict might arise.

That can happen only to the extent that the
persons who populate the arena, and in particular
the leaders, are secure in themselves such that
their personal integrity and well being is not in-
vested in their ideas being "the winners". It is

that kind of freedom that we find in Christ, the ability to risk ourselves in the free expression of truth, come what may, knowing that God Himself requires our belief in Him *only* on those grounds, and that God is willing to risk our faith in Him on that basis. If God is so willing to risk our faith in Him on those grounds, we ourselves can do no less.

Only if these basic rules of the search for truth are allowed and if the Christian community has done its homework on this level, so that we know what our fundamental commitments are, we know what identifies us as Christians, we know what is important and what is peripheral to our faith, can the pastoral level of engagement be carried out with any stability. Love and communion cannot happen in chaos.

There is nothing esoteric about this business. It is a mystery to be shouted from the housetops. It can be very scary, because we are risking everything that our trust in Jesus as King of kings and Lord of lords is indeed reality, the intellectual side of the way of the cross, if you like. We are taking that monumental leap into believing that truth really will set us free. But we need to do it just the same. That is the way a God of history and of a sacramental creation reveals Himself. It is the way God has chosen to include all of us.

The rules of the arena of truth seeking are those which are applicable in every walk of life, no matter how simple and unsophisticated. As Christians learn to practice truth seeking and truth living at all levels of their lives, they will become what God intends, His Body on earth, the present reality of the life of God, visible, tangible, the new Adam and Eve, made in His image, male and female.

J. Inclusiveness in the Dialogue

The Christian community is committed in principle to finding the truth about sexuality and living in it. It is also committed to obedience to the will of God. There have been times when those two goals seemed to diverge. One must express gratitude to any group of persons who attempt to clarify those issues for us, and who present the

case as best they can to ease that stress by bringing empirical evidence and the will of God into
conformity. The forgoing thoughts have been offered hopefully to work with the diocesan commission toward that end.

But we sit, whether we like it or not, on our
three-legged stool of Scripture, personal experi-
ence/reason, and tradition. The dialogue, if it is
to have the integrity of being a dialogue *of* a
viewpoint *with* a viewpoint, must take place *from*
those established legs. The report and the liberal
thrust today has been to tell us that our already
confirmed positions are not valid while the debate
is proceeding, that we must suspend our given positions, balance on two or one, or perhaps even no
legs, while we are re-examining our viewpoints.

But the fact is that the Church does have a
position on the moral issues being contested. It
is legitimate to challenge that position, but the
burden of proof falls heavily on those who say that
an agreement and understanding of over 20 centuries
affecting the fundamental nature of the Church and
its message is to be abandoned for a different
stance.

With that in mind and in view of the preceding,
criticisms of the report might be raised in three
areas, with the intention of moving the dialogue
further on toward a mutually helpful and satisfying
conclusion. If such dialogues ever conclude. The
three areas I would point to are 1) the standards
for deciding what is and is not "Biblical", 2) the
relation between science and Christian faith and
practice, and 3) in some ways most importantly of
all, the dialogical process itself.

The report would benefit from clearer standards
by which we as a Christian community could discern
between Biblical and non-Biblical. What do we include and what do we exclude, and how do we decide?
Since much of the discussion is over that very
issue, to continue the dialogue without some clear
understanding if it would seem to consign ourselves
to running in circles. That is indeed the deeper
issue at stake, not sexual morality. Perhaps we
need a diocesan commission to explore the meaning
of the word 'biblical'.

The report would also benefit from a more accurate understanding of the relation between the scientific enterprize and Christian religion. When science is assumed to be "the way to truth", and then pitted against any other set of practices or beliefs, Biblical or otherwise, science will of course always come out the winner, and we will not have a faith within which to include or exclude anyone. But that is not the relation science has to the Christian faith. Until we come to understand that relation, we Christians will find ourselves pulled in two directions, between Christianity and truth, not, if you are a Christian, a comfortable place to be.

The report offers itself, in correspondance to stated diocesan policy, as a part of the dialogical process on the matters at hand (p. 38), a process meant to be an inclusive one. A dialogue, however, requires two. The best way to encourage a dialogue is to be openly involved in one. The report gives the mistaken impression, however, of having issued from unanimous commission agreement on substantive issues, an agreement which was not in fact true of the commission. Twice the report suggests that there might be disagreement on the commission (p. 5, 38), but never is there any serious thought given to letting the reader know the nature of that disagreement or what the basis for it might be.

The intent of the report is stated:

> We intend...to report on the issues with statements
> of opinion and recommendation that we believe re-
> flect legitimate Christian ethical positions.

But only a very narrow range of opinions is allowed into the report, and those are given the full weight of scientific backing in a manner that does not bear inspection. Further, specific opinions that have been held by Christians for centuries are dismissed. Regarding homosexuality, for instance:

> Such persons have often been called sick or sinful,
> but these portrayals cannot be considered diagnos-
> tic. (p. 19.)

Presumeably that is thought to be so because the American Psychiatric Association some years ago removed the label "homosexual" from its diagnostic listings. The APA, however, was not unanimous in that decision, it is not "the Voice of Science", and in any event does not speak for the Body of Christ. Dr. Quentin Hyder, in a letter to the *Darien News-Review*, 1/7/88, wrote:[42]

In December 1973 the board of trustees of the American Psychiatric Association (A. P. A.) voted to change the category of homosexuality in their diagnostic manual to "sexual orientation disorder." The manual then directs that this diagnosis should only be used if the patient's "sexual interests are directed primarily toward people of the same sex *and* who are either disturbed by, in conflict with, or wish to change their actual orientation." In other words the board in their collective wisdom decreed that "homosexuality per se is not by itself a psychiatric disorder because a significant proportion of homosexuals are apparently satisfied with their orientation and are able to function as effectively as heterosexuals."

Contrary to these views a minority group within the general membership of the A. P. A. petitioned to restore the category of homosexuality to the manual. While agreeing that all social injustices inflicted on homosexuals were deplorable the petition affirmed the widely held view that homosexuality is an outcome of conflicts beginning in early childhood, and as such *is* an appropriate subject for psychotherapeutic intervention. It stated that it is a disorder of psychosexual development which is learned experientially. In other words it is a developed habit.

For this reason it is scientifically fallacious to assert that individuals are disturbed only if they cannot adjust to homosexuality. Many of them are disturbed by the very pathology which caused the misorientation in the first place. The petition continued with the assertion that homosexuals generally *do* suffer from multiple intrapsychic anxieties which cause them to develop an aversion from potential opposite-sex partners. Although they indeed might be able to function well in the employment arena, they have an extreme impairment in functioning in their private lives because they are unable to fulfill their sexual role appropriately and "in accordance with anatomy and biological reality."

---

42 See above, section G, "Objective Human Nature".
    For a further insight into this matter of the APA decision, see Ruth Tiffany Barnhouse, *Homosexuality: A Symbolic Confusion*, Seabury Press, (Winston), N. Y., 1977. Ms. Barnhouse is a psychiatrist and theologian in the Episcopal Church.

Homosexuality therefore *is* a psychiatric disorder and should be regarded as a medical illness which can be successfully treated if the patient is cooperative. What makes it different from most other illnesses however is the fact that it is usually the direct result of voluntary acts over which the patient had full control. Hence therefore the moral issue.

.... Attempts to show an endocrine gland imbalance involving sex homone deficiencies have had little success. There is also no proof that homosexualiy is an inherited genetic abnormality. Both these lines of investigation have yielded much controversy but few facts. ....

It is very rare to meet a truly happy homosexual. The majority suffer from a variety of concomitant neuroses sometimes directly related to their orientation. Almost all manifest some degree of depression, loneliness, anxiety, shame, guilt, feelings of inferiority, helplessness, inner conflicts, unfulfilled desires, and a craving to love and be loved which can rarely be satisfied by a lover with similar, as opposed to complimentary, anatomy. Stable homosexual relationships are relatively rare, and faithful commitment to one partner is uncommon. By contrast, promiscuity, and therefore potential exposure to infection and disease, is very widespread.

Finally it has been my experience in almost 25 years of psychiatric practice that homosexuality can be effectively treated on the one essential condition that the patient is highly motivated, and truly desires to change. This motivation can be either religious, moral, social, or hygienic .

Edward Eichel, family and marriage counselor, comments on the political agenda behind the APA's decision in his paper on "heterophobia", the section entitled, "The 'Denormalization' of Heterosexuality - Politics of the APA Decision".[43] The decision, he contends, was part of an effort by groups such as the Kinsey Foundation who believe in a "pansexual" philosophy, not only to make homosexuality an acceptable alternative to heterosexuality, but to foster the position that heterosexuality is a deficient or even neurotic kind of behavior.

---

43 See the following article, "Science - The Poisoned Well", in which I quote extensively from Eichel's paper.

There is clearly a position that has not been audibly heard. The spirit of dialogue and truth-seeking requires that *any* position be put on the table for discussion, certainly those positions which have been long and deeply held, and not dismissed with a wave of an alleged "scientific" hand. Since the position that homosexuality might involve either sin or sickness is dismissed, no mention is made either of organizations of ex-gays and heterosexuals who are ministering to those gays who want to become heterosexual. A whole range of very legitimate Christian thought and activity is ignored.

The inclusion of a "minority report" would have given the commission's report far deeper substance and sense of reality about the issues that actually confront Christians. As observed above, comments are made occasionally about those who propose "easy answers". One might note that the "easiness" of an answer in the bad sense is not a reflection of its being either simple or clear, but of its lack of realism and truth, and of the process of honest dialogue and confrontation with alternative answers. The report would toughen up its own answers by allowing and encouraging that sort of dialogue to happen.

These issues were not invented by either the *Newark* or the *Connecticut Report*. They have been with us for decades, as have Kinsey, Masters, and Johnson, whose work we will examine in the following article. There is nothing in either report that has not been debated by Christians for some time, with the possible exception of some recent medical developments. But there have been some vigorous responses to this "pluralism" which have been dubbed "knee jerk" as though the responses were ill thought out and not sensitive to what was being proposed. Nevertheless, when someone takes an ax to one's foot, one's knee might be expected to respond spastically.

The Christian faith rests on the three-legged stool of Scripture, tradition, and personal experience and reasoning about the experience. If an ax is taken to any one of those legs, then the stool is in danger of collapsing. The thrust of much of the argument of the two reports has the effect of undermining not only the role of Scripture and tradition, but of reason itself, for the acid effect of the perennial philosophy operates not only on sacred writings and sacred tradition, but on the very integrity of our ability to live in reality through which those sacred texts and traditions were developed. All three of the legs of the stool of faith, including reason, are in danger. And if the process is not challenged, Christians will indeed find themselves without a leg to stand on, or a knee to jerk. (The amputation was a success, the patient died.)

If this picture is true, then one must suspect that science itself lies in danger, for science is utterly dependent on a notion of a real, objective world and on methods for getting at knowledge of that world. The same drift toward relativism that threatens the Church leaves no part of our world-view unscathed, including the scientific part, a matter to which we turn in detail in the third article of this series.

III.

SCIENCE

THE POISONED WELL

Preface

This portion I have written to be included in the present work only with reservations. Because of its sensational nature, it may distract from some other issues that demand perhaps even more attention. My hope is that the following will not distract but point to and underline the importance of the issues of sexuality in relation to our spiritual and scientific communities. Much of what is to be described could never have happened had the Judeo-Christian community in western culture been in a healthy relation to the scientific community. It seems rather that the same evil has infiltrated both communities.

The events outlined below point to the fountainhead for much of the "perennial philosophy" already discussed to find its way into western culture under the guise of "truth" and "science". We zoom down from the wide angle lense and general issues of the previous articles to narrow focus and a very particular issue, source, and wellspring, and a particular group of scientists.

That we are engaged in spiritual warfare, not polite and disinterested academic discussion, will perhaps become evident if it has not already. The perennial philosophy is the pseudo-philosophy of the world in ignorance of and/or in rebellion against God. It purports to seek truth but leads into endless confusion and contradiction both in the theoretical and in the practical and moral realms. I occasionally give a two hour lecture diagraming and illustrating the nature of the perennial philosophy, which I precede with the warning that "this might be one of the most depressing two hours of your lives". The worldly may like to "whoop it up" and give the illusion having a successful pursuit after the good things of life, but when the issues are laid bare, it is clear that those who live in the world really are people without hope.

The material that follows documents one of the most sordid chapters of that worldly story, the blossoming of an evil in America over the last forty years which the armies of Hitler and his axis powers could not accomplish.

In the fall of 1987 I was given some material by a fellow parishioner who was himself deeply involved in bringing sanity to his local school sex education scene and who knew that I was working on the development of a Biblical view of sex, psychology, and human nature. The material consisted of 1) a paper, *Public Policy Implications of the Kinsey 1948 "Child Sexuality Data"*, based on material given by Dr. Judith Reisman in 1981 at the Fifth World Congress of Sexology in Jerusalem, 2) a letter by Mr. Edward Eichel directed to the president, ethics committee, and board of directors of the American Association of Sex Educators, Counselors, and Therapists (ASSECT), and 3) an article, *Heterophobia - A Hidden Agenda in Sex Education?*, by Mr. Eichel and J. G. Muir.[1]

Mr. Eichel's letter was a formal complaint alleging that

> a "pansexual" agenda is being promoted by gay activists which has no foundation in science and is destructive to the health and well-being of the general public. The agenda follows the Kinsey tenets that (1) <u>bisexuality is the norm of sexual health</u>, and (2) that <u>pedophile relations are beneficial for children</u>.
> Most disturbing is the evidence that teacher training is being directed toward targeting school children for the above agenda.

---

1 Mr. Edward Eichel, M.A., is a human sexuality, marriage, and family life education consultant and a certified psychotherpist, with offices at 463 West Street (A-1106), New York, NY 10014.

    Dr. Reisman holds a Ph. D., is president of The Institute for Media Education, and may be contacted at Box 7404, Arlington, VA 22207. Her article is excerpted from a book currently in preparation, *Child Sexuality or Child Abuse? -- A Critical Analysis of the Kinsey Reports*.

    It is with the authors' permission that I quote extensively from both papers.

The two articles by Dr. Reisman and Mr. Eichel document these allegations by Eichel from Kinsey's own writing, and give evidence which any interested person can check for accuracy for the most part simply by visiting his local library to read the work of Kinsey and others referred to in the articles, or the offices of, for example, SIECUS[2] to ascertain their philosophy, or in many cases by digging into the sex-ed curriculum material of one's local school system. I would add also Planned Parenthood to the list of organizations one might visit for an eye opener.

Neither of the articles have as yet found publication, although both Reisman and Eichel have made continued efforts to find publishers. Both have experienced the frustration of their work being accepted for publication, and then at the last minute having the publisher withdraw support. It seems clear to them that vested interests get knowledge of the content of their work and apply appropriate pressure to prevent publication. This pressure to curtail the free exchange of information and views (censorship) is nothing new to the media and publishing industry, but it appears to be a policy which one finds consistently entrenched in so many areas of the current discussion of sexual morality. There is a dogged unwillingness to allow the traditional viewpoint on sexual morality to find a place of free expression in the arena of debate, and that despite protestations of "open dialogue" and "inclusiveness".

The deeper one looks into the situation, the more one tends to conclude that in many cases of those promoting, for example, public school "sex education" courses, the alleged interest in assisting young people in handling their sexual problems, curtailing the growing epidemic of promiscuity and unwanted pregnancies, and bringing order to the chaotic sexual scene is simply false. There is clearly a non-public agenda. The brazen conflict between on one hand spoken words of good intent and on the other hand behavior which can only lead to the opposite of the alleged intent, namely the increase, not decrease, of sexual disease and discomfort and immorality is fair warning of dishonesty and power struggle alien to the realm of honest science.

---

2 Sex Information and Education Council of the U. S. (Not a government organization.)

A. The Well and the Poison

In the preface to this book, I express having
had a puzzlement over so many persons having
"bought the secular baloney" that God is either
dead or never existed. The suspicion seems to un-
derlie our cultural mentality that this new found
knowledge had been brought about by the rise of
science, of which we all learned in history class-
es. The theory of science leads one to believe
that scientific institutions and scientists who man
them are dedicated to "the truth, the whole truth,
and nothing but the truth...."

Western civilization has been drinking deeply at
the well of science for over three centuries, and
with truly astounding success in those matters to
which scientists legitimately addressed themselves.
In its own appropriate realm, the rise of science
has changed the shape of human affairs in a way
second to none at any time in human history. And
it would have been good that we drank so deeply,
had not someone poisoned the well.

There has not been, as secularists would sometimes like to picture, an unmixed blessing in the
draught from this well. We have seen science
co-opted by forces which rival any in history for
sheer brutality, hate, and insensitivity to anything but their own will. It has not been only
technology, the fruit of science, but theoretical
science itself that has been co-opted, with all of
its authority for "truth saying". "If 'science'
says it, it must be true", has become the well nigh
impregnable position of the scientist. Anyone desiring to persuade the population would do well to
heed such power and authority. Some heed it by
seeking and saying the truth, and others heed it by
clothing themselves in the garb and paraphernalia
of science to look like they are saying the truth.

Some, that is, want to have all the authority of
scientific persuasion without having paid their
dues under the discipleship of truth-seeking and
truth-saying. That discipleship means first of all
having removed from one's interest in science any
personal investment of ego or identity or desire
for power or prestige or success. If one is interested in the truth for its own sake, that means he
has no agenda which he is not willing to put on the

table for public inspection, and that his personal ego needs are met *apart from* his success in the realm of scientific research and application.

The secularization of science meant that those engaged in science no longer had God, who stood outside of natural science because He stood outside of the world of nature, in whom to invest their ego needs. If their lives were not to be "hid in Christ", where would they be hid? They, however, neglected to provide a suitable substitute, and proceeded on their way assuming that they could handle things on their own. The result has been the continual and inevitable backsliding of the scientific venture into the control of vested interests and the selling out of science to persons who had more interest in having their way than in truth speaking. Science has become, by and large, the pawn of various forms of power politics, a matter to which Allan Bloom refers in his discussion of the American intellectual community.[3]

Inspired originally perhaps by Sigmund Freud, the field of sexology has tried to establish itself as a scientific discipline. One would hope in this deep and sensitive area of human welfare to find the highest sense of truth seeking and truth speaking, and the highest devotion to human welfare. But a research into the history of the matter, as Edward Eichel and Judith Reisman show, would appear to indicate otherwise.

The work of Kinsey and his associates in the field of sexology is the main target of Eichel and Reisman, but Kinsey himself was working with a background which was to a large degree Freudian. Freud believed, as did many at that time, that human nature could be interpreted by models taken from the physical sciences. His notion of "drive" was an adaptation of the nature of physical energy and force with which physicists worked. It was, and is, a model which, as we have said, if misused, effectively snuffs out a sense of freedom and purpose in human life, and therefore makes moral effort meaningless.

---

3 *The Closing of the American Mind*, Simon Schuster, New York, 1987. See especially, Part Three, The University.

Kinsey did, however, split from Freud on one significant issue, the very issue of Reisman's and Eichel's papers. Whereas Freud believed that heterosexuality was the normal mode of sexual expression, Kinsey proposed a "pansexual" ideal. Wardell Pomeroy, one of Kinsey's co-authors, referred to Kinsey's work of converting not only the sex education field but all humanity to the alleged freedom of pansexuality as Kinsey's "grand scheme".

"Unisex" is the pop version of pansexuality, the more or less undefined sense that males and females do not have any significant differences of gender beyond the constraints of hard, physical biology. "Pansexuality", however, is a sophisticated and far reaching theory of sex which holds that there is no such thing as a true heterosexual situation, that is, there is no real polarity in the normally imagined heterosexual sense between the masculine and the feminine. Province I of the Episcopal Church held a conference in Holyoke, Massachusetts in November, 1987, under the title, "An Exploration of Intimacy, Sexuality and the Church". At the conference, John Fortunato, psychotherapist and author, who described himself "as a gay, non-militant Episcopalian", articulated very clearly a portion of the pansexual position:

> "Male/female dichotomy is not the basis of marriage," he said. "Commitment and faithfulness which help each partner grow are the important ingredients."[4]

Fortunato is opting for a view of human nature in which the essential inner distinctions of masculine/feminine are discounted as non-essential. One might want to agree with him that we are first of all persons before we are males or females, but one cannot leave the matter at that point. The masculine/feminine dynamic is an essential, non-optional part of the fleshing out of personhood. When Paul notes in Galatians (3:28) that in Christ "there is neither male nor female", he is not saying that either Genesis 1:26 ff. or the significance of being a male or a female has been dispensed with, rather he is talking, as the context clearly shows, about the fact that we are accepted into the Kingdom of God as persons, not as males or females. *Within* the Body of Christ, according to Paul, male/female roles still obtain, as expressed

---

4 *The Living Church*, November 20, 1987, p. 6-7.

in Ephesians 5. And throughout Scripture, the masculine/feminine roles are used to picture the relationship between God and His people.

According to the pansexual view, whether we are biologically males or females, we are all somewhere on a spectrum between the two in a manner that makes it perfectly proper for me to seek sexual satisfaction, i.e. orgasm, from any stimulus, male or female, animal, vegetable, or mineral. Kinsey followed Freud in the belief that sexual orgasm was the primary pleasure and goal of the human species on the grounds that we humans are essentially animals, and from the Kinsey point of view, sex is the primarily activity and goal of all animal life. Kinsey writes,

> Freud and the psychoanalysts contend that all tactile stimulation and response are basically sexual, and there seems considerable justification for this thesis, in view of the tactile origin of so much of the mammalian stimulation.[5]

But whereas Freud condemned adult-child sexuality as "abnormal", "cowardly", and a "substitute" outlet for "impotent" people, Kinsey affirmed rather that orgasm by any one stimulus was, for all practical purposes, as good as any other.[6] That the stimulus might be a child or an animal or an object made no significant difference, and certainly not a moral difference. As Kinsey said,

> It is...difficult to explain why each and every individual is not involved in every type of sexual activity.[7]

The source of stimulation was essentially irrelevant so long as it produced the orgasmic state of feeling. Freud introduced the notion of child sexuality, Kinsey went further to produce "hands on" evidence to "verify" the matter, as we shall see. Many of Kinsey's major conclusions such as the above quote were based in part on the material in

5 Alfred Kinsey, *Sexual Behavior in the Human Male*, p. 163. W. B. Saunders, Co., Philadelphia, 1948. Kinsey shows in this comment his belief that the human species was simply a high form of animal life. His sexuality does not include any serious moral or spiritual content.

6 Sigmund Freud, *Three Essays on the Theory of Sexuality*, ed. and trans. J. Strachey, (New York: Basic Books, 1962), pp. 14-15. Originally published in 1905.

7 Alfred C. Kinsey, Wardell B. Pomeroy, Clyde E. Martin, and Paul H. Gebhard, *Sexual Behavior in the Human Female*, Saunders, Philadelphia, 1953, p. 451.

chapter five of his *Sexual Behavior in the Human Male* (1948), in which he describes his experiments on pre-adolescent males. It is strongly suggested that the reader obtain that book at the local library and peruse chapter five in particlar.

The importance of Kinsey's position, and the influence of the Kinsey Institute, can hardly be over estimated in western culture, and especially in America. Morton Hunt describes Alfred Kinsey as sexology's patriarch in his *Sexual Behavior in the 1970's*:

> ...Dr. Alfred C. Kinsey...was the giant on whose shoulders all sex researchers since his time have stood. Those who participated in the present project used his data, his thoughts and his words every day until we supposed them our own....[8]

One does not need to be a sexologist to be aware of the impact the Kinsey reports, with their affirmation of a pansexual human nature, have had on the popular imagination. I recall the flurry of furtive excitement and curiosity my last year in high school in 1953 when *Sexual Behavior in the Human Female* was published. And I recall asking myself, out of mixed outrage, curiosity, and surprise, a very proper and scientific sort of question, "How does he know all that stuff? What kind of a laboratory does he have, anyhow?" Nearly three and a half decades later, thanks to Reisman, Eichel, and a reading of Kinsey, I am finding out.

One wonders what would have been the result had Kinsey come out with two books which put the whole weight of scientific approval and credibility behind a strongly Biblical position, emphasizing the rightness of a heterosexual stance, chastity, and life-long, monogamous marriage as the appropriate place for sexual expression. We would not have the present influence of the Kinsey Institute, and probably also not the consortium of other groups and institutes, including Planned Parenthood, SIECUS, etc. The "sex revolution" of the '60's and '70's might have been profoundly different. One does not want to attribute more influence than is factual, but it would be hard to imagine those decades proceeding down the same path without the backing of something like the Kinsey Reports and

---

8 New York, Playboy Press, 1974, see acknowledgements. See also Reisman's article, section entitled, "Who Educates the Sex Educators?"

the influence of those groups who so powerfully
backed the pansexual restructuring of our attitudes
toward sexual behavior.

During those decades, I had assumed, as did most
of us, presumably, that being a *scientist*, he was
of impeccable credentials. He must have known what
he was doing, and who was I to question him? And
so I conveniently explained away those unpalatable
items of the Kinsey reports. If that was by a
stretch of the imagination an excuseable response
on the part of a layman in the field, it was not an
excuseable response on the part of the profession-
als. The impact of an unexamined and unquestioned
- until recently - sexology on the American mind
has been little short of staggering. It might well
be that the Freud-Kinsey-Masters-Johnson development of sexology, more than any other single factor, contributed to the virtual demolition of the
Judeo-Christian sense of sexual morality in America, and perhaps western culture. And all this done
in the name of objective science. It is this latter assumption of scientific objectivity which
Eichel and Reisman are challenging.

The adoption of a materialist notion of sexual
activity, that is to say, a notion which was rooted
in biology devoid of any significant spiritual
value and very little psychological or moral value
beyond, "Does it feel good," was an inevitable development from certain aspects of the Freudian
school. This materialism is that primary collapse
of God into the world which is the chief characteristic of the "perennial philosophy", bringing right
with it the third characteristic, the collapse of
objective morality.

The development from Freudian materialism into a
pansexual scheme was simply an inevitable matter of
time. For once the sense of an objective rightness
and wrongness falls, once there is no longer an
objective standard by which "behavior appropriate
to" a male or a female can be measured, the measure
has no place to rest but in one's own private feelings. Freud was indeed a moralist, but his morality was little more than a leftover from the rubble
lying all about him of the Judeo-Christian cosmic
framework. Such a morality could only appear "culturally determined" at best (it had to be because
the superego was culturally determined), and would
soon fall before the advancing ranks of the cultural and anthropological relativists. (As well it

should, for Biblical morality was never meant to operate outside of the Biblical cosmos.) But sexuality must then of necessity gravitate into narcissism, the psychological mother of solipsism, the philosophical version of absolute and total self-absorption. Pansexualism thus illustrates the fifth characteristic of the perennial philosophy, the drive toward total personal autonomy and self-sufficiency.

The following is an extensive quotation from Reisman's paper, the section entitled, "The 'Child Sexuality' Data", which in turn quotes directly from Kinsey's *Sexual Behavior in the Human Male*, in particular chapter five dealing with his research on pre-adolescents:

> In Chapter Five of *Sexual Behavior in the Human Male*, Kinsey *et al* claimed to provide the scholarly community with the first scientific data proving that children both desire and benefit from genital sex with adults and peers. This data came from recorded measurements of adult stimulation of hundreds of children, two months of age to nearly 15 years old. The Kinsey team alleged that the smallest infant and child subject responded well to their genital stimulation by experimenters. The team noted the advantages to children of this type of activity:
>
> > [T]here are cases of <u>infants</u> <u>under</u> <u>a</u> <u>year</u> <u>of</u> <u>age</u> <u>who</u> <u>have</u> <u>learned</u> <u>the</u> <u>advantages</u> <u>of</u> <u>specific</u> <u>manipulation,</u> <u>sometimes</u> <u>as</u> <u>a</u> <u>result</u> <u>of</u> <u>being</u> <u>so</u> <u>manipulated</u> <u>by</u> <u>older</u> <u>persons</u>... When an older person provides the more specific sort of manipulation which is usual among adults, the same child may be much aroused, and in a high proportion of cases may be brought to actual orgasm (chapter 5) [Reisman's emphasis][9]
>
> "Advantages" of "specific manipulation" (genital stimulation) for up to 24 hours (around-the-clock) were presented.[10] "Stopwatch" measurements were used by "trained observers" to derive the following information from the child sex experiments: "Speed of pre-adolescent orgasm", "time between orgasms" (measured in minutes and seconds), "numbers of or-

---

9 Kinsey, et al, *Sexual Behavior in the Human Male*, p. 501.
   See Reisman, "Public Policy Implications of the Kinsey 1948 'Child Sexuality Data'", section entitled, "The 'Child Sexuality Data'".

10 Ibid., p. 180, table 34.

gasms" in a given time, and so on. At least 28 of the experimental subjects were identified by Kinsey, *et al*, as one year of age or younger.[11]

* 32% of children under one year "achieved" orgasms. The number rises to 57% in 2 to 5-year olds.[12]

* one 4-year old was "specifically manipulated" for 24 hours around-the-clock, "achieving" 26 orgasms in this time period.[13]

* One 11-month old infant, apparently under manual or oral manipulation (See Gebhard letter) was "observed" to have 14 orgasms in 38 minutes, or 2.7 "orgasms" per minute.[14]

* One 13-year old was "observed" having three orgasms in 70 seconds, or one "orgasm" each 23 seconds.[15]

These and other elaborately detailed data on several hundred infants and children are presented in tables 30 through 34 in Chapter Five of the Kinsey Report, *Sexual Behavior in the Human Male*. Who conducted these child sex experiments, and for what purpose, will be addressed shortly.

First, the Kinsey team admitted that the child subjects endured "prolonged varied and repeated stimulation".[16] They also stated that this stimulation was provided by "technically trained" experimenters.[17] How, then, did the team describe the child subjects' responses to such stimulation? The team described six types of child reactions, some of which were:

---

11 Ibid., p. 176, table 31.

12 Ibid.

13 Ibid., p. 180, table 34.

14 Ibid. Also see personal correspondence with Dr. Paul Gebhard (March 11, 1981), past president of the Kinsey Institute for Sex Research (now called the Kinsey Institute for Research in Sex, Gender and Reproduction). A letter to Dr. Reisman accompanies her paper, in which Paul Gebhard, in 1981 the director of the Kinsey Institute, replied to some questions by Dr. Reisman.

15 Ibid., p. 180, table 34.

16 Ibid., p. 178, paragraph one.

17 Ibid., p. 177, paragraph one.

* Extreme tension with violent convulsion; often involving the sudden heaving and jerking of the whole body...gasping, eyes staring or tightly closed, hands grasping, mouth distorted, sometimes with tongue protruding; whole body or parts of it spasmodically twitching...violent jerking of the penis...groaning, sobbing, or more violent cries, sometimes with an abundance of tears (especially among younger children.).

* ...Hysterical laughing, talking, sadistic or masochistic reactions....

* ...extreme trembling, collapse, loss of color and sometimes fainting of subject....[18]

While pediatricians would claim that collapsing, twitching, convulsing and fainting children require medical attention, the Kinsey team interpreted these behaviors as an expression of children's "pleasure". [19] This unusal view of pleasure is further magnified in the team's final description of child orgasm:

Pained or frightened at approach of orgasm...sometimes males suffer excruciating pain and may scream if movement is continued or penis even touched. The males in the present group become similarly hypersensitive...will fight away from the partner and may make violent attempts to avoid climax, although they derive definite pleasure from the situation.[20] [Reisman's emphasis.]

Pediatric opinion verifies the logical conclusion that children in the conditions described above were held or tied down during some of the experiments. Moreover, those children who failed to respond to these conditions with "pleasure" were evaluated by the team as probably psychologically impaired:

The observers emphasize that there are some of these pre-adolescent boys...who fail to reach climax even under prolonged and varied and repeated stimulation. But even in these young boys, this probably represents psychologic blockage more often than physiologic incapacity.[21] [Reisman's emphasis.]

---

18 Ibid., p. 161, number 3.

19 Ibid., numbers 5 and 6.

20 Ibid., number 6.

21 Ibid., p. 178, paragraph one.

How did sex scientists reach conclusions about children's sexual response based upon the testimony of the children's sexual exploiters? By analogy, would valid data on female sexual response be collected from rapists who described their victim's "pleasure" during rape?

Two issues emerge from such an exploration into Kinsey's efforts to enlighten us on matters of sexuality: first, the fact that his work has the appearance, at least, of having involved criminal sexual assault on children and infants; and secondly, the matter of the philosophical position which apparently justified such behavior in his own mind, in the minds of his colleagues, and even more surprisingly, in the minds of so many ordinary citizens-at-large who read his works. If the picture of Kinsey's sexology given above, quoting directly from his own words, be true, how could it be that for nearly four decades, this was accepted without question as scientific work of high and unquestionable quality, done in the service of the human race?

As unbelievable and painful as the treatment of young children apparently was, a matter which needs further and fuller investigation, we also need to know what in a man's mind provides the justification for such behavior when the standards believed in for centuries stood firmly against such activity. And that is the issue I wish to address, for it is this very "justification" which has been operating *sub rosa* in many ways throughout our culture, including within the ranks of Christians and the deliberating rooms of the Church.

If the basic ontological assumptions of Kinsey are true, that we are essentially biologically formed and determined beings, and that sex is not a moral issue, if there is no "behavior appropriate to" a male or a female, no objective standard for masculinity and femininity, then the very meaning and substance of life must necessarily revolve around one's own private feelings. If physical reality is the essential reality, if the world is a closed system without recourse to God, then contact with the currents and energies of that reality, for humans through their bodies and through their sexual capacities, clearly becomes a very important matter.

If therefore, sexual energy, imagined as mechanical drives, are inherent within the human being from birth, and if a (perhaps even THE) primary goal of life, is the experiencing of these energies flowing through one's being, then clearly anything that gets in the way of that happening is not a good, but a bad. If my basic ontological foundation is like Freud's "libido", an undifferentiated sexual drive, perennially thrusting upward into my conscious out of the depths of the subterranean realms of my unconscious, constantly seeking its fulfillment, that is, its pleasure, then the "good" of life will be to set that energy free to have its way. And then social constraints which hinder this flow of sexual energy through me in my quest for union with my deep inner physical nature will be my enemy, not my friend. The picture is a classic expression of the materialist version of the closed circle, self-contained, self-sufficient universe, divine, substantial in and of itself, the primary characteristic of the perennial philosophy.

And that is the picture presented by Kinsey. Freudian psychology has the advantage, like Janus, the Roman god, of looking in two opposite directions, a matter of some discomfort to Freudians who occasionally dispute on which direction is the "real" Freud. Freud's notion of a libido which surges upward from the unconscious to assert itself in the conscious life, the ego, was obviously in need of a governing force, which Freud called the super-ego. The superego emerges from pressures of the obvious and (more or less) realistic constraints of communal living. There are other egos and other libidos besides my own trying to express themselves in the world. For any of us to survive we must learn to get along. The necessity of social living and the expectations put on us by family and society are what create the superego within us. It is largely through the authority of the superego that the drives of the libido are sublimated (literally, made sublime, raised up out of the murkiness of the raw unconscious).

But that is precisely where Janus looks two ways. Some Freudians side with the freedom of the libido, others with the necessity of discipline for communal living. For those who side with the libido, sublimation is not "making sublime", but rather accepting second best in place of the real thing. Genital sexual pleasure sublimated into art, industry, and other forms of creativity are only pale reflections of orgasm, the primary and "real" pleasure. On the other hand, for those who look in the social direction, pure libido is only raw material that must be refined into the higher (more sublime) forms of culture and society.

Kinsey clearly opted for the libido drives and their free expression. Kinsey acknowledges the existence of social constraints, but seldom does he mention them in a context where they are any more than neutrally recognised. Social constraints would at best be there to protect our ability to pursue the real sexual pleasure. And more often his language suggests they are a negative force. "Social values", "social taboos", "social restrictions", and the like are pictured as getting in the way of full sexual development. According to historian Paul Robinson regarding Kinsey's "homoerotic model":

> He evaluated every form of sexual activity in terms of its role in the sexual lives of the lower species, and he frequently concluded that outlawed sexual practices were entirely natural because they conformed to "basic mammalian patterns"...[including] sexual contacts between human beings and animals of other species.[22]

Reisman notes:

> Robinson points out that Kinsey, et al, were anxious to prove that all sex acts and behaviors are only "outlets", thus, fully natural. He documented the Report view that "...all orgasms were equal, regardless of how one came by them..."[23]

> Again, if all sex were merely "outlets", infants could enjoy orgasms with "older persons".[24]

And Eichel:

22 Paul Robinson, *The Modernization of Sex*, New York, Harper and Row, 1976, p. 56. See also Reisman, section entitled, "Sex Science Influence in Sex Offender Policies".

23 Reisman, section entitled, "Sex Science Influence in Sex Offender Policy", see also Robinson, op. cit., p. 59.

24 Reisman, op. cit., section entitled, "Sex Science Influence in Sex Offender Policy". See also Kinsey, et al, *Sexual Behavior in the Human Female* (1953). See for example, pp. 167, 170, 173; also *Sexual Behavior in the Human Male* (1948), pp. 160, 167, 170, 177.

The Kinsey group (which included Wardell B. Pomeroy, Clyde E. Martin, and Paul H. Gebhard) defined their concept of sexual normality as follows, "...we suggest that sexuality, in its biologic origins, is a capacity to respond to any sufficient stimulus."[25]

Since the Kinsey group does not suggest that there are any origins other than the "biologic" ones, one must conclude that that ends the matter for them. Eichel relates a tell-tale comment dropped by Kinsey:

Finally, there is the issue of Kinsey's lack of concern for the emotional implication of sex acts as reflected in a comment he made to Pomeroy in response to criticism about their research - "Now, they want us to consider love," he said. "If we started on that, we'd never finish."[26]

Had they started with love, they never would have *begun* their kind of research.

Eichel makes reference to an "instruction kit" which "introduces young people to orientations other than heterosexuality" entitled *About Your Sexuality*, including filmstrips "explicitly depicting erotic acts between homosexuals and between lebians":

The late professor Deryck Calderwood of New York University, who developed the program under the auspices of the Unitarian Universalist Association, stated his rationale for the recently revised 1983 edition. "There has...been a change in the way 'Love Making' is approached." He elaborated, "In the present version all love making is placed in one unit." [Previously there were separate units on heterosexuality and homosexuality.] "Now, however, the material focuses on the human experience of making love first, and looks at the choice of partner as a secondary one."[27]

---

25 Eichel, op. cit., section entitled, "Basic Errors in Sex Research". Also see Kinsey *et al*, "Concepts of Normality and Abnormality in Sexual Behavior," in *Psychosexual Development in Health and Disease*, ed. P. H. Hoch and J. Zubin (New York: Grune & Stratton, 1949), p. 27.

26 Eichel, op. cit., section entitled, "Basic Errors in Sex Research". See also Wardell B. Pomeroy, *Dr. Kinsey and the Institute for Sex Research*, New York, Harper and Row, 1972, p. 105.

27 "Explicit Sexual Materials - Useful Tool for Education of Teenagers," an interview with Deryck Calderwood in *Sexuality Today*, Vol. 7, No. 50, October 1, 1984. See also Eichel, op. cit., section entitled, "The SIECUS Principles for Sex Education".

It is striking how one can word an unsavory matter to appear noble. The material focuses, that is to say, on feelings first rather than on persons. Persons are denigrated to the level of tools for producing feelings. We begin to see relationships as instruments for feelings rather than feelings as perceptions of relationships.

There is a traceable link, I believe, on one hand between a trinitarian theology and a hetero-sexology, and on the other hand between a unitarian theology and a pansexology, as suggested above by the link between Calderwood's work and the Unitarian Universalist Association. A unitarian theology will tend to blur distinctions within *human* persons in much the same manner that it will blur distinctions within the *divine* person and image, in which image we are made, and perhaps for the same reasons. It is a move which tends to atomize personal relationships and to diminish our sense of interdependence and communal life. We tend increasingly to resemble billiard balls knocking around on a table with no internal connections, rather than a deeply inter-related and inter-connected community. And moral values lose their reason for existence, namely to structure the ontological framework of the community in and through which we exist.

Kinsey does not say or imply that there might be any goal in sexual intercourse other than a pure feeling experience. The way to the "divine" is through feeling experience devoid of intellectual or objective moral content, the third and fourth characteristics of the perennial philosophy. Parents and society who get in the way of freely experiencing orgasm are pictured as restrictive and rigid.[28] The difference between experiencing freely and experiencing promiscuously fades into the mist.

Such a view of sexuality implies that sexual intercourse is *not essentially a relationship*, a mutual sharing of lives, a giving and a receiving, and certainly not a sacrament in the image of God. The other person is there not for any value in and of him- or herself, but rather simply as an instrument for pleasure, a stimulus. Who or what the stimulus is matters little other than for its effectiveness in being pleasure productive. In fact

---

28 Kinsey, et al, *Sexual Behavior in the Human Male*, see pp. 164, 171, 173, 174, 177, 178.

the existence of *relationship* gets in the way of
the emergence of true libido expression, for relationship is exactly what produces the forces of
superego, i.e. having to take into account someone
else's needs and wants, and therefore possibly having to forego a pleasure of one's own. The inherent gravitational drive is clearly toward narcissism.

It would be difficult to find a clearer and more
precise or a more deliberately and knowingly pursued expression of the pampered-child life style
than the pansexual "grand scheme" imagined by the
Kinsey program. As Alfred Adler wrote of Freud's
psychoanalysis:

> Its transitory success was due to the predisposition
> of the immense number of pampered persons who will-
> ingly accepted the views of psycho-analysis as rules
> universally applicable, and who were thereby con-
> firmed in their own style of life.[29]

If feelings are taken as ends in themselves, one
is necessarily impelled into narcissism, the ab-
sorption of oneself into one's own feelings, a
state which does not allow for the reality or legitimate expression of the feelings of others. But
if feelings are seen *as perceptions of relationships*, then it becomes clear that feelings cannot
realistically be pursued for themselves, and that
the only way to guarantee good feelings is to first
guarantee good relationships. That is the manner
in which God guarantees His Kingdom. The pursuit
of feelings in the manner of pansexualism is the
pursuit of pseudo-relationship, trying to produce
the *fruit* (feelings) of good relations without having taken *responsibility* for good relations.

Pansexualism is not merely adding "another dimension" to the heterosexual domain. The pansexual
view sees a heterosexual orientation as deficient
and lacking because it arises out of the constraints of society to put the human animal into a
limited box, the heterosexual box. True sexuality
is open to any and all sexual stimuli, and therefore the heterosexual who limits himself to the
opposite sex, or even worse, to a life long, monogamous relation, must be engaged in a deficient and
possibly neurotic form of sexual expression.

---

29 Alfred Adler, *Social Interest: A Challenge to Mankind*, Faber & Faber, London, 1938,
   p. 36.

B. The Babylonian Captivity of Science

Martin Luther wrote an impassioned treatise entitled, *The Babylonian Captivity of the Church*, to express his deep dissatisfaction with the sacramental system of the Roman Church.[30] His allusion, of course, was to the Babylonian captivity of Jerusalem. Babylon is in the Biblical world a major symbol for the world system in darkness, ignorance, and rebellion against its Creator.

Science has been for the greater part of the last one hundred years in almost total captivity to secular materialism, modern Babylon, the view that matter, not God, is the ultimate reality, to the point that many scientists have felt ashamed to express a relilgious faith in public. The notion that "science" knew more about life than did God, or than God at least was able to communicate to us, was sold with great persuasion to the populace at large, including to large segments of the Christian community. The "hard core" of secular psychology has been behaviorism, which has wanted to interpret human nature in machine-like terms, reducing all data as nearly as possible to the readings of gauges, dials, and other physical measuring instruments, and exorcising any ghost of purposiveness from the subject at hand.

The five marks of the "perennial philosophy" are present in secular science in general and in pan-sexology in particular: 1) the collapse of God into the cosmos, 2) the failure of objective truth, 3) the demise of objective morality (there being no purpose to things), 4) the obsessive concentration on feeling at the expense of intellectual input, 5) and a consequent obsession with autonomy and independence from relationship.

Masters and Johnson in 1966 published their study, *Human Sexual Response*, a work which stood on the shoulders of Freud and Kinsey in its fundamental assumptions about human life.

The impression has been created that Masters and Johnson researched and defined *the nature of the sex act*. In *Human Sexual Response*...the research team concluded that orgasm had the same basic response patterns regardless of whether the stimulation was

---

30 See Martin Luther, *Three Treatises*, Muhlenberg Press, 1943.

human or mechanical.[31] The theme was expanded in
Homosexuality in Perspective (1979), in which they
proclaimed that, "the inherent facility for sexual
'attainment' is identical....regardless of whether
the sexual partner is of the *same* or *opposite* gender."[32] These findings appeared to provide a
physiological basis for Kinsey's pansexual viewpoint. It didn't matter what you did, or who you
did it with.

Certain parts of Masters' and Johnson's conclusions, for example, were drawn from sexual experimentation done with electronic and mechanical devices, based on the assumption that intercourse for
a man or a woman with a physical object, in this
case an electronic sensor, is in all essential respects the same as intercourse with, say, one's
spouse.[33] In this they simply followed Kinsey's
pansexual program in which any sufficient stimulus
was as good as any other. Curiously enough, "sufficient" is measured in contradictory ways, on one
hand, in terms of production of pure, raw feeling,
and on the other hand, in terms of the results
obtained on gauges, dials, and other mechanical
devices, two very opposite ways of looking at
things.

One does want to congratulate behaviorist psychology on its creative and imaginative explorati-
ons of human sexuality, but one does also wonder
whether either Masters or Johnson made the comparison themselves between the machine and the warm
body. It may be that Masters' and Johnson's electronic devices could detect only "the same basic
response patterns regardless of whether the stimulation was human or mechanical", and that the
gauges and sensors could find no difference between
a stimulating machine and a stimulating human
being. So much the worse for the gauges and sensors. One would be hard put to sell this total
reduction of sexuality to mechanical stimulation of

---

31 William H. Masters and Virginia E. Johnson, *Human Sexual Response*, (Boston: Little,
  Brown, 1979), pp. 133-4. See Eichel, op. cit., section entitled, "Basic Errors in
  Sex Research".

32 Masters and Johnson, *Homosexuality in Perspective* (Boston: Little, Brown, 1979), pp.
  404-405. See Eichel, section entitled, "Basic Errors in Research".

33 A mechanical device was in one instance used because vaginal response is unable to
  be monitored when a live male is involved, it not being possible to insert an
  electronic sensing device and the male organ at the same time. In this contest to
  see who is the best "sensor", the live male loses.

feeling devoid of personal relationship to many married couples. The ultimate "sensor" will still *in every case* be a person, not a machine. If subjective "feeling" is really so totally determinative for the value of sexual experience, then it is difficult to fathom why one should remain so glued to dials, gauges, and electonic sensors. Clearly there are some deep contradictions afoot.

Kinsey was aware that he was treading on dangerous legal ground with his research. He ventures a comment, reflecting both his acceptance of behaviorist materialism and toward the relation between research and social constraint:

> Erotic arousal is a *material* phenomenon which involves an extended series of physical, physiologic, and psychologic changes. Many of these could be subjected to precise instrumental measurement if objectivity among scientists and *public respect for scientific research* allowed such laboratory investigation.[34] [Fox emphasis.]

If erotic arousal is *only* a material phenomenon so that there are no moral or spiritual aspects to consider, then of course it is beside the point for the public to object his experimentation.

Reisman writes:

> When secrecy becomes a part of a research effort, it is irresponsible for critical readers to give investigators the benefit of the doubt.... Pomeroy said:

>> No aspect of sex...was a matter for disdain as far as Kinsey was concerned....[35] In this conflict between his scientific zeal and the strictures of society, Kinsey [and his team] characteristically decided in favor of science.[36] [The team was]...acutely aware of the serious dangers implicit in such work and proceeded cautiously, knowing that [they]...could expect little understanding of what [they were]...doing if it was ever disclosed.[37] [W]e were prepared to destroy the records and throw ourselves on the mercy of the court.[38]

---

34 Kinsey, *Sexual Behavior in the Human Male*, p. 157.

35 Pomeroy, W. B., *Dr. Kinsey and the Institute for Sex Research*, p. 122.

36 Ibid., p. 172.

37 Ibib.

38 Ibid., p. 141.

Pomeroy charged that Kinsey would "...have done business with the devil himself if it would have furthered the research".[39]

The extraordinary fact is that Kinsey and his team have never had to "destroy the records". They might have hidden their work while in progress, but they apparently did publish both their methodology and their conclusions in very clear English thirty nine and thirty four years ago respectively for the two "Kinsey Reports" on males and females. So in one sense, they cannot be said to be guilty of deceit, unless one counts as deceit clothing very volatile material in sterile "scientific" language. It was not hidden away discreetly in some occult archive nor in the decent obscurity of dead Latin. It was available for all to peruse. Why was Kinsey *et al* never seriously and successfully challenged in the American imagination?

They were not challenged, it would appear to me, because American culture had already digested and assimilated a large part of the perennial philosophy. It had already so far lost its moorings in the Judeo-Christian worldview that when the frontal attack came, garbed in the white coat and clinical atmosphere of "science", we were simply and literally stupified. We could not, until recently, raise one single effective voice in protest because we, or most of us, even in the Christian community, had secretly suspected that neutralized, steriziled, secularized "science" really did know more about such things than we (or God) did.

In the meantime, the perennial view, quite happy to don the high priestly robes of the "scientific investigator" (with an "infallibility" aura equal to any pope or fundamentalist), continued deftly and skillfully to remove the ground right out from under the Biblical worldview.

Christians tended to drift in either of two directions, to retreat further into defensive "infallibility" positions, or to accomodate faith to the "new age". We were not willing to give up our faith, but we did not feel we had solid ground upon which to engage the enemy because, with only a very few exceptions, we did not know how to deal with either philosophy or science. We did not understand the true relation between the Biblical faith and either of these.

---

39 Ibid., p. 198.

There is only one way for anyone to "deal with" philosophy or science, and that is to get into them, find out what they are and what truth they have to offer. If Christians do not do that, *others will*. And Christians will be left looking rather lame because, being ignorant of the real issues, they will not be able to discern legitimate use of science or philosophy from false, deceitful, and manipulative uses.

A paramount illustration of the latter is the attempt to pass "science" off as a kind of "neutral ground", free of philosophical or theological commitments (or anti-commitments), where "objective" people can get together to discuss the real issues. Those who have a moral or theological commitment are not welcomed into the discussion because they are "biased". The role that Kinsey and many others have tried to play, thinking of themselves as objective scientific observers standing outside and above the moral realm, is patently false. They have had an agenda which was in fact a behind-the-scenes-frontal-attack on the Judeo-Christian moral viewpoint, the main inspiration for which was not legitimate science but a moral (or an anti-moral) philosophy of their own. They knew right where to go for the juglar vein. As Eichel and Reisman show, their agenda cannot be said to have had the pure spirit of scientific objectivity behind it.

Eichel notes that SEICUS[40] and the Kinsey Institute, with links to the National Institutes of Mental Health, are deeply involved in the current drive to influence and/or provide sex education in our public schools. Eichel then asks:

> What then is on the horizon? In their article "The Future of Sex Education" in the *Journal of Sex Education and Therapy* (Spring/Summer 1985), SIECUS co-founder Dr. Lester Kirkendall of Oregon State University and Dr. Roger Libby of the University of Massachusetts predict that sex education of the future "will probe sexual expression...with same-sex [partners]" and "even across... generational lines." They proclaim that with "a diminished sense of guilt....these patterns will become legitimate" and "the emphasis on...normality and abnormality will be much diminished with these future trends."

---

40 Sex Information and Education Council of the United States (not a government organization).

"Across generational lines" opens the doors for "acceptable" incest. And then:

> If the protective bond that exists between parent and child could be broken down, the boundless vision of changing sexuality presented by Kirkendall and Libby might be more likely to become a reality.
> .... There is evidence of a tactical focus on young people and an attempt to *direct* their sexual choices, independent of parental influence and societal norms.[41]

Eichel then makes reference to the North American Man/Boy Love Association (NAMBLA) which produced a document, "Resolution on the Liberation of Children and Youth", advocating "that children 'must have the unhindered right to have sex with members of any age of the same or opposite sex...'" Dr. Theo Sandfort, whose book, *The Sexual Aspect of Paedophile Relations*, was initially banned in the United States,[42] concludes as Eichel suggested:

> It can be expected that when the boundries around the nuclear family disappear, children will more readily accept emotional ties with adults other than their parents.[43]

"Accept emotional ties" does not, of course, mean merely "being friendly", it means "have sex with". Given the close relations between the many groups associated with the Kinsey Institute,[44] it is not far fetched to assume a commonality of philosophy, goals, and strategy, and that a very powerful consortium is at work to achieve these ends. It would not be far fetched to assume that much of the tendency in America today to diminish the role of the nuclear family is inspired by the Kinsey approach and the Kinsey "team".

The burden of "developing guidelines for an accrediting body for university-based degree programs in human sexuality" was taken on in 1983 by the

---

41 Eichel, op. cit., section entitled, "The SIECUS/NYU Programming -- Bisexuality & Pedophilia".

42 Amsterdam, Pan/Spartacus, 1981. See Eichel, op. cit., section entitled, "The SIECUS/NYU Programming".

43 Eichel, op. cit., section entitled, "SIECUS/NYU Programming".

44 See Eichel, op. cit., esp. diagram opposite table of contents.

Society for the Scientific Study of Sex (SSSS).[45]
This is a standard and necessary procedure for any
newly developing branch of knowledge. But it is a
process which of necessity requires openness to the
various different viewpoints that might be engaged
in that particular field. One would want to ask
whether the Judeo-Christian viewpoint is being invited to express itself in the implementation of
this accrediting procedure. Eichel notes that
Deryck Calderwood from NYU, Kenneth D. George from
the University of Pennsylvania, Wardell Pomeroy,
former Kinsey co-worker, and Paul Gebhard, one time
director of the Kinsey Institute were members of
the original accreditation committee:

> All of these academicians are committed to the
> "gay"-oriented, Kinsey-school ideology.[46]

Eichel again:

> It is doubtful that a gay lifestyle could have
> gained the "currency" it has acquired in the last
> few decades, even with the influence of the Kinsey
> reports, if it had not gotten intermingled with is-
> sues critical to the heterosexual community. It was
> Mary S. Calderone who gave the gay activists in
> SIECUS the benefit of credibility she had amassed in
> her years as medical director for Planned Parent-
> hood. Under the SIECUS banner sex education was
> linked to a gay agenda. When Calderone "retired"
> from SIECUS, she joined Calderwood as an adjunct
> professor in his NYU program. SIECUS has now moved
> to New York University.[47]

There is nothing suspicious about one group
being "linked" to others. That is the nature of
groups and of the advancement of knowledge among
groups. Neither is it pernicious to try to foster
one's agenda through such groups. That is how any
agenda, even God's, gets fostered. But it does
help to know just where a given sex philosophy is
coming from and what its honest credentials might
be. When in this case, the pieces of the moral and
philosophical and scientific and political puzzle
get put together, the picture appears to emerge of

---

45 Eichel, op. cit., section entitled, "Accreditation for Human Sexuality Programs --
   Standardization of the Kinsey Ideology". See also *The Society Newsletter* (SSSS),
   May 1984, under the caption "National Committees 1983-84". Names of committee
   members are listed. The accreditation process began in 1986.

46 Ibid.

47 Eichel, op. cit., section entitled, "The SIECUS Principles for Sex Education."

a very definite philosophy, well organized, trying
to commandeer the scientific community and its rep-
utation for "truth seeking" in order to give credibility to a way of life that would otherwise have
been totally unacceptable to society at large.

Over the last two decades as the move to establish sex education programs in schools met with
resistance, one heard of "those fundamentalists"
interfering with the educational process. And I
wondered myself what the furor was about, being
aware of how ultra-conservative groups can inhibit
legitimate progress. "We do need to know the facts
about sex, don't we?" I thought. Some of the hor-
ror stories seemed overly reactionary until I personally sampled some of the material being used.
No doubt there are paranoid persons reacting un-
helpfully to the circumstances, but there are also
very real circumstances to which sane and rational
people should be firmly and decisively reacting.

Reisman writes:

> The Kinsey pansexual network has monopolized the
> accreditation of university human sexuality pro-
> grams, influenced the training and certification of
> health field professionals, and influenced the
> planning of professional conferences. Further, the
> network has, with outreach programs, guided the edu-
> cation of sex educators and sex and family thera-
> pists, and has carried its doctrine into a broad
> spectrum of other fields, including theology and
> justice. By circumventing public and scholarly
> criticism and censure through the use of fabricated
> data which could not legally be replicated, the Kin-
> seyan sexual ideology was accepted by default, and
> has become an article of faith in academic sexology.
>
> The field of sexology must clear its name before
> the law, science, and society. ....the Kinsey
> statistics may have been utilized primarily to sup-
> port a personal vision that had little to do with
> objective scientific research.[48]

According to Eichel,

---

48 Reisman, op. cit., section entitled, "Re-evaluating the Kinseyan Ideology".

In pursuing their agenda, the pedophile movement has attempted to capitalize upon the period of parental conflict that inevitably occurs as youths enter the difficult stage of their adolescent development.[49]

The desire to capitalize on the stress of teen-age growth may be a partial explanation for the strange behavior of so many who are pushing for "health" (i.e., sex) clinics in high schools and in even lower grades, to deal with the epidemic of unwanted pregnancies. There does not appear to be any indication that the establishment of such clinics has any result but to make matters worse precisely because of the refusal to deal with the moral issues involved. Passing out morally neutral technical information, the "what" without the "why", does *not* normally change behavior other than to encourage experimentation in that very information.[50]

> Since Kinsey believed that *hetero*sexuality is abnormal - simply a symptom of cultural repression, there would be no need to "change" the orientation of children. A "hidden" gay agenda in sex education would reach boys and girls before they are affected by societal "restraints", and rescue them from the supposedly pathologic norms of male-female relating.[51]

This capitalizing on parent-teen stress may also partially explain the bizarre behavior of so many in dealing with the AIDS crisis, even among Christians, refusing to recommend chastity as "the way to go" rather than promoting with a "condom morality" the very thing that needs to be stopped. What can explain the stubborn refusal, when the lives of people are at stake, to affirm chastity, a monogamous, life-long relationship, as behavior appropriate for both males and females?

Another part of the strategy would appear to be an active, if disguised, proselytising for the bi- or homosexual viewpoint. Eichel describes in his

---

49 Eichel, op. cit., section entitled, "The SIECUS/NYU Programming -- Bisexuality & Pedophilia".

50 See, for example, *Effects of Family Planning Programs on Teenage Pregnancy*, presented by Stan E. Weed, Ph. D., from the Institute for Research and Evaluation to the U. S. Senate Committee on Labor and Human Relations, Senator Ted Kennedy, Chairman, July 28, 1987.

51 Eichel, op. cit., section entitled, "The SAR (Sexual Attitude Reassessment) Seminar -- For Professional Certification".

letter to AASECT, and refers to in his paper,[52] "nude body workshops" in which participants of the same sex were instructed physically to explore each other's genital organs. Eichel raises the issues as to whether this is part of a "heterophobia" program designed to create interest in homosexuality in potentially impressionable persons. The nude body workshops were part of the Deryck Calderwood instruction developed as a part of the NYU Human Sexuality Program, which in turn would partially qualify one as a trainer of persons who would teach sex education courses in the public school system. One wonders whether this might be described as an attempt to create an emotional addiction to homosexuality, much as a drug dealer draws persons into the heroine habit by passing out free samples. Any process that introduces one to a pseudo-relationship, good feelings apart from responsibility for good relationship, will have the potential of creating an addictive dependency.

One seems forced to conclude that sexual stability is not the aim at all, that indeed instability is the goal as a part of a campaign to attain an ulterior end, the justification and establishment the "grand scheme". When one promotes a program ostensibly to lessen promiscuity and unwanted pregnancies and venereal disease, but then refuses to do those things that really would help lessen them, and promotes activities and teachings that make them in fact inevitable, one might be led to assume that deceit and lies are being perpetrated.

The AIDS crisis has often been compared to the bubonic plagues of the middle ages. Thousands are dying from it, there is no known cure, and yet one hears very seldom, at least through the media, of leaders firmly standing on the side of the only moral position with an ounce of credibility. One has to wonder what sort of mind operates from such a position, such that it is willing to risk countless lives to promote a "grand scheme" that has neither solid scientific, nor philosophical, nor spiritual backing for it, but was rather by its very nature a private, narcissistic scheme imported into the scientific realm, and which has all the appearance of being pursued to justify and undergird the authors' own life style.

---

52 See section entitled, "The SIECUS Principles for Sex Education -- A Declaration of Abnormality?"

Reisman writes:

> The confirmed criminality of Kinsey's subjective "observers", and the complete absence of a mechanism for verifying the experimental research findings are reason alone to reject Kinsey's conclusions.[53]

The obvious reason for the "absence of a mechanism for verifying" the Kinsey research is that to verify Kinsey's work would involve criminal activity, that is, the sexual abuse of children and infants. It is not "abuse", of course, from the pansexual point of view, rather it is introducing children to the joy of life. And it will not remain "abuse" on the legal books if the pansexual team has its way.

And that is the issue. Kinsey's view that his investigations have proven the legitimacy of his pansexual program are false, not only because of the shoddy scientific procedure, but because before that procedure even began, the traditional moral position had already been written off as unworthy of consideration. The spiritual and moral issues were simply ignored, with "science" the alleged ground for the rejection of moral standards.

What science can discover about sexuality, as we have discussed, is the limits and range of its possibilities, what it can and cannot do. Science is not in a position to discover by itself what it is *for,* the goal and purpose. The pansexual agenda has already decided, in conformity with the "perennial" program, that it is for *feeling, devoid of either intellectual or moral commitment*. "If it feels good, do it," an accurate motto for the perennial/pansexual program.

That sexuality needs to be scientifically investigated and that some of the work of Freud, Kinsey, Masters, Johnson and others can be of value is not to be questioned, insofar as they were indeed producing scientific data within the bounds of acceptable moral behavior, that is, data which can be legally and morally replicated and verified. But it is also clear that serious questions need to be raised concerning the scientific, philosophical, and moral integrity of much of their work.

Eichel writes about the "victim" strategy of the gay rights movement:

---

53 Op. cit., section entitled, "No Replication Legally or Morally Possible."

In conclusion, a basic issue must be brought to the attention of the public - are gay activists waging a campaign against heterosexuality *per se*? And, indeed, against the long held societal taboo on adult-child sex? A one dimensional picture has been presented that homosexuals are victims of discrimination and their civil rights are constantly being threatened. There is little or no attention given to the possibility of transgressions against the heterosexuals - even children. The strategy underlying much of the rhetoric about gay rights has been defined clearly enough by a historian of the gay movement, Dennis Altman, in his book, *The Homosexualization of America*:

> The greatest single victory of the gay movement over the past decade has been to shift the debate from behavior to identity, thus forcing opponents into a position where they can be seen as attacking the civil rights of homosexual citizens rather than attacking specific and (as they see it) antisocial behavior.[54]

The fact that this ploy could have been, and still remains, so effective is an illustration of the extent to which the Christian community has lost its own Biblical grounding. The difference between "who I am" and "what I do" is one of the foundation stones for understanding the Gospel of Jesus Christ. To try to "be myself" or to "be a somebody" *through what I do* is what the New Testament would call "salvation by works". The basic substratum of "who I am" is something I receive from God, a gift, a matter of grace, not something done or earned. "What I do", not "who I am", is the arena in which conviction and repentance take place. The fact that this confusion was able to be perpetrated upon Christians is evidence of the inroads of secularizing within the Church. Had the Christian community been firmly grounded on this point, no one would have been able to turn aside an honest assessment of homosexual behavior by the reply that someone's being or identity was under attack, for making an assessment of one's behavior does not *ipso facto* imply an attack on their identity or being.

---

54 Eichel, op. cit., section entitled, "Gay Rights -- The 'Victim' Strategy".

C.   The Spiritual Battle for Science

We have taken a long detour, it might seem, from
the subject of the *Newark Report* and *Connecticut
Report*, into Freud, Kinsey, Masters, and Johnson.
But the detour has taken us right to the heart of
the matter, that is, to those sources to which both
the *Connecticut Report* and the *Newark Report* make
appeal, namely to the *science of sexology*. And
indeed, one finds in the two reports strong echos
of the methodology and philosophy of the Kinsey
program, and both the Kinsey program and the two
reports reflect elements of the perennial philosophy in contrast to the Biblical worldview.

It would be unfair and untrue to say that every
sexologist or sex therapist in America subscribes
to Kinseyan pansexualism, or that the writers of
the two reports were consciously determined to support an anti-Biblical viewpoint. But it would be
accurate to say that the pansexual program with all
of its related institutional networking, has had an
extraordinary and unfortunate effect on the American imagination, and that this effect has worked
powerfully on the minds of many Christians in dealing with issues of human nature. This effect is
clearly evidenced in the two reports we have been
considering.

If the picture given by Eichel and Reisman is
true, as the writings of the pansexual proponents
themselves would seem to indicate, then western
culture has been drinking deeply at a poisoned
well, and we have experienced and are experiencing
a prostitution of science equal to that of Nazi
Germany in its disregard for human welfare and its
degradation of personal values. It is small wonder
that the "teenage rebellion" years, often a time of
some stress, have become a major trauma for so many
families, that we are experiencing an epidemic of
runaway children, often caught up into the smut and
pornography industry, that divorces have escalated
to the 50% mark, and that teen pregnancies and
abortions have steadily risen in the last two
decades, coinciding with the very years of the rise
of the "pansexual" dream, secular, amoral sex-edu-
cation programs, and school health (sex) clinics.

One wonders what kind of statistics the public needs to see that we have taken a wrong route. What kind of proof is required to make us change our minds about the way we are going? The rational response to things getting worse during a program which purports to set things right is to say that the program was evidently wrong. But what we hear instead is, "Let's have *more*. We have not yet gone far enough." What is wanted is more technical education about sex, as though that would forewarn students of the dangers ahead, but devoid of information on the purpose of sex and the moral and emotional and spiritual commitments they are making even if they are unaware of it.

Some disasters have to be seen to be believed. The reader is strongly urged to investigate his or her local school system to see the actual teaching materials, videos, textbooks, etc., which are being used. Such materials are accessible under the freedom of information law. Government funds which are denied to religious bodies are being given to pansexual groups operating under the guise of objective scientific research to promote programs which are in fact "religious" in the sense that they are backhandedly anti-religious and attempting to be a replacement for Biblical religion.

The disaster is couching at our door. Pansexualism is a malignancy quite at home in our culture, destroying literally millions of persons. It has to be one of Satan's most powerful and effective tools in all the history of mankind. It has been offered to us in scientific, intellectually respectible, morally permissible, psychologically healthy wrapping. But when the cover is removed, we see raw sewage looking much more like naked rebellion against God.

The casualties are rolling into counselors' offices from over two decades of permissiveness. One gets weary of the yawns and eyes raised heavenward that greet the suggestion of moral issues as significant to psychological growth and health. Narcissism and simple inability to "grow up" are replacing Oedipal-type conflicts as the major symptom of emotional disturbance. And yet the Church itself continues to follow in the footsteps of the world's drift, exhibiting an unbelievable insensitivity and lack of compassion to the needs of our culture and time, let alone to the voice of God. Moral stability in the sexual realm is one of our

clearest and most obvious needs. The failure of
the Church to mark out a clearly delineated moral
stand indicates the lack, not the presence, of compassion and sensitivity.[55] We are dealing with
a sexual moral issue in the Church but also with an
even deeper *pastoral* moral issue, the failure of
our pastors to speak the truth to their flock.

And much of this tragedy is rooted in the mis-
conception that science is behind the "new morality", that there is a body of scientific evidence to
support the contention that chastity is no longer a
valid moral requirement. The evidence is not
scientific, but rather the prejudgement of an un-
vindicated personal philosophy. It is a judgement
which issues from a specifically materialist
framework which therefore makes any other conclusion impossible. That in itself does not make Kinsey and his conclusions wrong, but it says that the
issue is not a scientific one. Rather it is a
philosophical and theological one, and the philosophy and theology will have to stand on their own
feet.

Kinsey writes:

....it must be accepted as a fact that at least some
and probably a high proportion of the infant and
older pre-adolescent males are capable of specific
sexual response to the point of complete orgasm,
whenever a sufficient stimulation is provided.[56]

Apart from the apparently criminal methods used
to ascertain these "facts", Kinsey's argument is
founded on his narrow materialist definition of
'specific sexual response' and 'complete orgasm'.
If these are assumed to be *only biological* func-

---

55 In a pastoral letter to the Episcopal Church dated October, 1987, entitled, "The
Presiding Bishop's Message on AIDS", the Rt. Rev. Edmond Browning rightly called
for support of ministry to AIDS victims. The bishop also made remarks that might
be interpreted as denigrating the traditional moral teaching on the subject. He
then noted that "we are being called home to the basic tenets of our faith," but
made not a mention of that tenet of our faith which *everyone knows, because it is
common and uncontested knowledge*, is the only currently effective prevention
against sexually transmitted AIDS, namely sexual chastity, monogamous, life-long
relationship.

At the 1987 annual convention of the Episcopal Diocese of Connecticut, one of
the display booths was passing out information on "safe sex", the use of condoms to
prevent contact with one's sexual partner's body fluids, *despite the knowledge that
condoms are estimated to have a better than 10% failure rate.*

56 Kinsey, *et al*, *Sexual behavior in the Human Male*, p. 181.

tions, then of course his contention might have
validity in the context of his materialist philosophy. But if, as seems the far more evident and
rational position, there are clear psychological
and spiritual components to a "complete orgasm",
then his contention that even infants can have
these experiences is simply false. To tingle a
child's nervous system, obtain spastic responses of
the sort that Kinsey describes,[57] and to call
that "complete orgasm" has to be the final *reductio
ad absurdum* of behaviorist psychology. Anyone who
believes such nonsense must be either the victim or
the perpetrator of a pathological contact with
human reality. It takes years of growth, discipline, and maturation to develop psychological
and spiritual responses in a mature relationship.
Any philosophy as destructive of personal reality
as is pansexualism is not only absurd and pathological, it is evil. The fact that we fall into believing such nonsense does not speak very well for
our cultural scientific objectivity or for our personal integrity. It says something very powerfully
about the fallen state of our human affairs.

We are not dealing with a "scientific" issue.
We are dealing on the much deeper level of basic
presuppositions about the nature of the cosmos, the
level of final and ultimate commitment. Science is
the issue in the sense that science has been used
by persons to gain credibility for their own not
otherwise very credible ends. We are struggling on
the level of spiritual warfare more than scientific
evidence, the issue of what is the world *for*? What
indeed is *science* for? Is science "for" anything?
Does it have a purpose? At this level the basic
issue is purpose, not scientific description. We
are struggling with the question, Who is in charge
of the cosmos? Is man really the center of all
things, the creator of all value? Does man himself
decide what science is for, or is there a Creator
of the world, and therefore of the possibility of
science, who has an opinion on the matter? Is
there a Creator before whom we are rightly held
responsible for the kinds of values we hold? Including scientific values?

---

57 Kinsey, *et al*, *Sexual Behavior in the Human Male*, p. 160-61. See above, section
entitled, "The Poison and the Well", Reisman's quotation from Kinsey describing the
response of children and infants.

The secular materialist camp has often wanted to co-opt science to its own corner, as though to say, "If you are not with us, you are not scientific." It has wanted to give the impression that the Judeo-Christian tradition was the enemy of scientific investigation, that is, of honest looking at the facts, whereas an honest look at history will not bear out that charge, neither historically nor philosophically.[58] The Christian community has committed its share of blunders, including some unfortunate attitudes occasionally held by *some* Christians toward *some* scientific issues. But it is not true to say that science and the Biblical worldview are by nature at odds.

It can be and has been argued that science would not have occurred had not Genesis 1:1 been written: "In the beginning, God created the heavens and the earth."[59] The existence of science as we know it (i.e. a search for objective truth about an objective world) is dependent on there being a clear separation between God and the cosmic order. It is exactly that separation of God from the cosmos which is the foundation of Old Testament religion, and which distinguished Biblical religion from the surrounding paganism. The devolution of current thinking into subjectivism and the loss of our grasp on objective reality, upon which science depends for its very existence, is rooted in the loss of our sense of the objectivity of a personal Creator and the re-collapse of God into the cosmos, as we have already discussed above.[60]

The more obvious issue of spiritual warfare before us is, "What is the purpose of sex?" But of equal or greater weight is the issue, "What is the purpose of *science*?" The warfare revolves around the answer to that question. Secular science has traditionally been the enemy of purpose in the cosmos, but the antipathy towards purpose in the cosmos does not come from science as such, but from the secularization of science. Either scientific enterprise will be used for the purposes and glory

---

58 See especially Stanley Jaki, *Science and Creation*, Scottish Academic Press, Edinburgh, 1974. Also, David N. Livingstone, *Darwin's Forgotten Defenders*, Eerdman's, 1987.

59 See Stanley Jaki, op. cit. Also my book, *Personality, Empiricism, and God*, to be available from Emmaus Ministries early in 1988. See endnote for details.

60 See above, *Inclusion and Exclusion - The Biblical Way*, section C, "Science vs. the Bible".

of man (science does have a purpose, but only of
our own making), or it will be used for the purpose
and glory of God. As an ultimate question it is
"either/or", there can be no compromise between
them. It would seem rather obvious that the fate
of the human race hangs on that decision, not only
in the area of sexuality, but of the military, of
politics, economics, culture, art, and any other
area one might name.

This warfare is not decided by scientific investigation, it is rather the arena of ultimate personal commitment, with the aid of whatever philosophy and theology one can garner. Science is, and
will always be, deeply in need of being rescued
from special interest groups advertising themselves
as the purveyors of objective knowledge when in
fact they have no such interest but only their own
bias. It can and does happen in the Church, but
the Church has no monopoly on bias and prejudice.
And the Church has a special commitment from an
Authority higher than any secular scientific establishment to maintain its integrity in truth seeking. Believers in God not only have peer pressure,
moderately effective at best, they have also to
stand before God for their honesty and truth-seeking and truth-sharing.

"Some disasters have to be seen to be believed,"
was the opening theme of Part I above, "Sexuality
and Family Life -- The Biblical Roots". But even
in the writing of that article there remained a
sense of fuzziness about "Where is this disaster
all coming from?" There is always, of course, simply our fallen human nature, our tendency to gravitate into the cheapest and easiest way, the part of
us that wants to be the center of our own world,
and that would really like to be a spoiled child.
I had been aware for over three decades of the
"perennial philosophy" and the many forms that can
take. But a philosophy is seldom specific enough
to get one's teeth into. My experience with the
pansexual material, on the other hand, although
sickening, was what I would imagine a fighter pilot
to experience as he looks up and sees the enemy
airplane dead ahead, fear and apprehension at
first, no more games and theory, and then glances
into his gunsights to see the enemy floating right
into the crosshairs.

The Christian is given only one offensive weapon, the Sword of the Spirit, which is the word of God (Ephesians 6:17), that is to say, the word of truth. The Christian must learn to expect the truth and to speak the truth, and in doing so to expose the falsehoods of the world in rebellion against God. If we learn to speak the truth in love, God will do the rest. The warfare is His, not ours, so that we can do our part in obedience, and let the rest fall where it may.

We are not engaged in *merely* an intellectual battle, but the battle does have a powerful intellectual component. The greater part of spiritual warfare is not exorcism, but honest truth learning and honest truth speaking and honest truth living. Christians must do their head homework. We must become able to articulate our own faith clearly and, as Abraham Lincoln was once heard to say at the end of a successful trial, "You have to know your opponent's case better than he does." We have to see what the "opponents" do not see, the pitfalls of their positions.

There is a spiritual war if only because the opponents are against spiritual things. But beyond the human flesh and blood level, we are dealing with "the principalities, ...powers, ...world rulers of this present darkness, ...the spiritual hosts of wickedness in the heavenly places." (Ephesian 6:12) We deal with such opponents through a deep life of prayer, and out of that prayer life, through responsible, step by step growth and sharing of truth in the circumstances around us

D. The Other Well -
Doing What Comes Naturally

Every Christian is responsible for the sharing of his faith with those in his or her circumstances, possible only if we know the content and rationale of our faith emerging out of a serious life of obedience to the Lord of our faith. We need to know the unique message that the Bible offers to the world, and to know the depth of that uniqueness. We need also to know and understand the world, *better* than those "in the world" understand it.

Christians need to understand and be able to
explain how the Biblical way of life offers a real
alternative to "the world's" way of doing things.
We need to understand that once one departs from
Genesis 1:1, certain consequences follow. Where
God is not taken seriously as the Creator of heaven
and earth the five characteristics of the "perennial philosophy" will soon be visible in the culture
which so departs. We do not need to badger anyone
into believing God or the Bible, but we do need to
be able to present it in clear and reasonable
terms. We need to let people know that Christianity cannot be subsumed and does not live under the
"perennial" or the "new age" or any other tent.
That is a matter of clear and demonstrable fact,
not of prejudice. Quite apart from whether the
Bible is true or false, the Bible is clearly saying
something *different*. Not until that difference is
seen are people really free to choose as to which
is true. The first job of an evangelist is to set
people free to choose, not to coerce a choice.

Knowing the world as God's creation means studying the world as well as Scripture. Natural science is a natural habitat for any Christian person.
Christians must therefore be involved in the legitimate study of human sexuality and be able to articulate the vision of the glory of God contained
in our being made in the image of God, male and
female. If that word from Scripture is true, then
the experience of sexual intercourse is in its own
unique way a participation in the image and likeness of God. It is a word which points clearly
toward a heterosexual understanding of human life,
not bi-sexual or homosexual.

I would not advocate a return to pre-pansexual
'40's and '50's. The greatest moral force (albeit
negative) of the 1940's was Hitler and his Nazi
party, who provided a scapegoat upon which to dump
our frustrations, an enemy against which to unite.
As a cultural force, World War II did far more than
the Judeo-Christian tradition to unite America and
to pull us up out of the doldrums of the Great
Depression. Whatever moral and spiritual unity we
possessed dissipated through the '50's, leading to
the public and private moral collapse of the '60's
and '70's, and the drift into the morass of "new
age" sexuality and morality and cosmology, of which
pansexualism is a major support. Today America

would be at loose ends without the "Communist threat" to find any sense of moral direction at all.

We must not move backwards to previous "golden ages" which had their own problems. We must move forward in our openness to the experience of life and reasoning about that experience, listening for the voice of God to open for us the paths of truth. The way forward is into a deeper and truer science, not into a fruitless and ridiculous battle against science. The way forward is a reconciling between the scientific and religious communities, who are after all, at least in principle, both wanting to understand the same "objective reality".

One must conclude from a survey of the literature that a clearly articulated heterosexual understanding of human life has not yet been developed by the science of sexology.[61] That branch of science appears to have been dominated not by scientific objectivity but rather by the perennial philosophy and a pansexual moral predisposition. If there is to be a scientific foundation to a Biblical morality, that foundation must include as one of its blocks the scientific development of a heterosexual understanding of sexual intercourse.

Eichel's research on the physical dynamics of intercourse provides the beginnings of just such an understanding.[62] His research points to the possibility, largely denied or ignored in most sexology today, of the male and female sexual response being a harmonious natural outcome of heterosexual intercourse properly learned. One of the primary complaints sexologists and family life counselors hear from married couples is that of the wife not experiencing orgasm at all, let alone simultaneously with her husband. The problem may have been compounded by the influence of Kinsey, who determined that

---

61 Mr. Eichel in a telephone conversation put me on to this thought with the comment that a heterosexual sexology had never been developed, that sexology has been developed to promote either a bi-sexual model of sexual "orientation" or or a pansexual spectrum of sexual behavior. That would go a long way to explain the extraordinary and puzzling conflict over sex education programs and the consistent polarity between such education and the Christian community. Sex is not the issue, but rather the clearly pagan presentation of it.

62 Inquiries on this research may be addressed to Mr. Edward Eichel, 463 West St., (A-1106), New York, N. Y., 10014.

the human male who is quick in his sexual response
is quite normal among the mammals [citing for example chimpanzees], and usual in his own species.

Kinsey contemptuously proclaims,

it would be difficult to find another situation in
which an individual who was quick and intense in his
responses was labeled anything but superior, and
that in most instances is exactly what the rapidly
ejaculating male probably is, however inconvenient
and unfortunate his qualities may be from the standpoint of the wife in the relationship.[63]

Married couples seeking counsel from sex or family therapists on the issue of sumultaneous orgasm
might likely be told that such an event was not
common, and not to pin their hopes on it being a
regular occurance if it occurred at all. Other
ways of "mutual satisfaction" would be suggested.
The emotional image created by such a thought cuts
right at the heart of the image of heterosexuality
as the norm for human sexual experience.

According to Eichel, however, new findings on
sexual response indicate that the experience of
simultaneous orgasm is indeed far more possible
than current sexology would lead us to believe.[64]
Furthermore, this truth can form the basis for a
much deeper understanding of the psychodynamics and
the spiritual import of the sex act, both of which
tend to be denied or trivialized in pansexualism,
and both of which have all too often been misunderstood, ignored, or denigrated contrary to Biblical
teaching but nevertheless in the Christian community as well.

Our basic sexual need is not in the final analysis physical, or a "drive" at all. It is rather
the spiritual need to unite within ourselves the
two sides of the image of God in which we are made,
the masculine and feminine. We need to get the
archetypal images of Father and Mother together.
We try mistakenly to "make it happen" by manipulat-
ing externalia, whether through heterosexual or homosexual activity, or through short cuts such as
pornography or sexual devices and self titillation.
But the inner unity can happen, as Eichel suggests,

---

63 Kinsey, *et al*, *Sexual Behavior in the Human Male*, Saunders, Philadelphia, 1948, p.
    580.

64 Inquiries may be directed to Mr. Edward Eichel, 463 West St. (A-1106), New York, NY
    10014.

171

not through conquering or seduction, but only through surrender to the objective reality of the "other". And likewise the external experience of sexual union can come only as a gift one to the other, ultimately from God, but mediated through one's spouse.

Because it is essentially a spiritual experience, the union of masculine and feminine within is necessary for celebate persons as well as married, and can be achieved quite apart from the married state or genital sexual intercourse. Indeed, it is out of the security of that "inner" marriage that the "outer" marriages can have reasonable stability. The inner marriage must come before we are capable of a truly adult experience of either celebacy or marriage.[65]

Pansexualism is held to be the "natural" way of doing things because, it is alleged, the libido, or whatever the sex drive might be labeled, arises naturally out of our physical selves or out of our psychic unconscious. And thus whatever that drive leads us to do is "natural" so long as it does not hinder another person in the pursuit of their self-expression. But the flood of books and articles purporting to assist one in his or her sex life give more the appearance of a somewhat desperate attempt to attain a tantalizing but ever elusive goal. The obsession with finding different and more exotic ways of "doing it" gives the appearance of an addiction rather than of "doing what comes naturally". There is a clear difference between what is natural and what is compulsive and addictive.

Addictive behavior has little touch with reason or with community living. It is self-centered and compulsive in its drive to establish a certain kind of feeling, whether through drugs, alcohol, sex, power, or money. It tends to use other persons as means to one's own good feelings rather than as valuable in themselves. A sexology which by its very nature is dedicated to producing pseudo relationships (good feeling, the fruit of good relationship, without the responsibility and commitment

---

65 See my cassette tape, "The Inner Marriage" (#D-2), dealing with our need to find our
    image securely in God in order to get the masculine and feminine aspects of our-
    selves in place. That inner marriage is a necessary part of any truly adult life.
    This tape is part of a series, "A Theology of Sexuality". See endnote on Emmaus
    Ministries for further information.

to that good relationship) will always lead into addictive relationships, which by their very addictive power will be experienced as "part of my built-in nature". The inability to deal with moral responsibility, however, will always be a tell tale giveaway that this is not a program for doing what comes naturally, but rather for doing what comes unnaturally, compulsively, and obsessively.

From the Biblical point of view, the fallen world is anything but "natural" and does not know how to do "what comes naturally". On the contrary, the fallen world, the world which has lost its essential relation of dependency and obedience to its Creator, is in a very unnatural condition. It is our nature to be in union with God, not in rebellion or ignorance of Him.

"Natural" sex, then, ought to be sex which is not unreasonable in its demands such that it overrides moral responsibility, but on the contrary sex which is the purposeful, positive, and cheerful fulfillment of moral responsibility. Natural sex will be sex which does not compulsively dominate but which is a cooperative aspect of one's life among many other aspects. It will be sex which involves neither "conquering" nor "seduction", but rather a mutual, cooperative, and willing self-offering.

Sex of that sort will of necessity proceed from an experience of personhood which is secure in its basic ontological dependency needs, a security which the world cannot provide. That means that sex itself, in its literal genital form, cannot be the *source* of that security, even though it might be one of the channels for it. Healthy sex will have to proceed from the kind of security which is found in the Biblical experience of salvation, the abundance of life of which Jesus spoke.

Edward Eichel, Judith Reisman, and others in the field of sexology, are aware of the need for a restoration of the Judeo-Christian cosmic framework and are pursuing in their sexology a scientific grounding for heterosexual relationship and monogamous life-long partnership as the moral and psychological norm for human behavior. Some of their material is on the verge of finding avenues for publication and will be available to the public shortly.

But the theological and psycholgical aspects of the matter are already available in easily digestible form. We have already in hand a "theology of hetero-sexuality" in a cassette album by that title.[66] The Christian community has never had in its history a clearly articulated theology of heterosexuality. The "hetero-" part has been, until the present era, for the most part gone assumed and unchallenged. But because we had no theology of sexuality in place, when the perennial pansexualism presented what seemed to be a clear science of sexology as a counter to the ill developed Biblical view of human nature and sexuality, the Biblical community has no response other than to quote the Biblical morality back at them.

It is not that the Biblical morality should not be quoted and indeed obeyed, but it will not appear very convincing if it is not backed up by a thorough going and well developed understanding of human nature, that is, a Biblical psychology incorporating sexology as a part of its presentation. No theory of the infallibility or authority of the Bible as the word of God will substitute for having done our homework in the realms of theology, psychology, and empirical science. When Biblical morality is quoted apart from a sufficient understanding of human nature, God tends to be seen as having issued arbitrary fiats which have little bearing on the lives we in fact live. But God had no such intention. His laws are the "operater's manual" given to make the gift of human life work most effectively and to accomplish that for which we were designed in the first place, not capricious whims of an insensitive cosmic Tyrant. We ignore them at our peril.

We are commanded in the creation story to "be fruitful and multiply, and fill the earth...." (Genesis 1:28) That's a lot of sex, and hardly a matter for blushes or prudery in Scripture. It is not the "forbidden fruit", and it is also not the "be all and end all" of human experience. It is simply what it is, primarily a way of manifesting

---

66 The cassette album, *A Theology of Hetero-sexuality*, including 12 tapes of a lecture series which I have given on Biblical sexuality, is available from Emmaus Ministries (see endnote for details). This material on cassette tape will be reproduced in book form. The first volume of that material, under the title, *Yahweh or the Great Mother? -- Man and Woman in the Image of God*, should be available in the summer of 1988, laying some of the basic foundations for the material discussed in the cassette form.

the image of God, and in that context God's way of getting new children into the world to be raised by us to become His children. It is only one of many ways in which the masculine/feminine unity is experienced or expressed, reflecting the unity within God Himself.[67] And genital sex is a mode of relating that is apparently not continued after the resurrection.[68] In any event, it clearly did not have for Jesus, or for any other Godly person in Scripture, the central and idolatrous focus which contemporary culture and pansexualism has given it.

The question will rightly be raised, "But where is compassion for the homosexual or the bi-sexual or the transvestite, or for those who are sexually active outside of marriage?"

It is folly to consider the question of compassion apart from the question of truth. If there is no objective truth, then compassion is whatever you want it to be. But if there is a real world with an objective nature, if there is a human nature which can be damaged by misuse,[69] if the Biblical picture of human nature is the true picture, then compassion consists in sharing that truth with any and all persons, and in assisting them to come to terms with the truth in as gracious and honest a manner as possible. Compassion does not consist in accepting kinds of behavior forbidden by God or which are in contradiction to a reasonable understanding of human nature. Such a response is misguided and shows lack of both courage and compassion for the genuine welfare of other persons.

Sex in the world is a fallen experience, like every other aspect of life.

"All things betray thee who betrayest Me",

echoes Christ, the Hound of Heaven.

---

67 See above, *Inclusion and Exclusion - The Biblical Way*, section E, "Sex and Gender in Creation".

68 That may be the meaning of Luke 20:35.

69 See my book, to be available in the spring of 1988, *Who Will Let Gene Out? - Biblical Inner Healing*, for a fuller development of human nature and especially of the unconscious processes and of how such processes can become damaged and healed. See endnote on Emmaus Ministries for details.

"All which I took from thee I did but take,
    Not for thy harms,
But just that thou might'st seek it in My arms.
    All which thy child's mistake
Fancies as lost, I have stored for thee at home:
    Rise, clasp My hand, and come!"

    Halts by me that footfall:
    Is my gloom, after all,
Shade of His hand, outstretched caressingly?
    "Ah, fondest, blindest, weakest,
    I am He Whom thou seekest!
Thou dravest love from thee, who dravest Me."[70]

Jesus told a woman in Samaria of a well from which we might drink which would pour forth with the abundance of eternal life:

> Everyone who drinks of this water will thirst again, but whoever drinks of the water that I give him will never thirst; the water that I shall give him will become in him a spring of water welling up to eternal life. (John 4:13)

It all comes down to as very uncomplicated, simple, non-philosophical choice -- Am I aiming for a self-centered, self-contained "my feelings are the only ones that count" attitude? Or, am I willing to follow Jesus on the way of the cross into true man- or womanhood?

> Jesus then said to the Jews who had believed in him, "If you continue in my word, you are truly my disciples, and you will know the truth, and the truth will make you free." (John 3:31)

If we do not respond to God's initiative in our lives and follow in obedience, we will not know the truth, neither about God nor about His creation, including the sexual part of it made in His image. We will know "truth" in only its most sterile, technical sense, and even that increasingly less as our grip on objective reality continues to erode.

Good feelings are the fruit of good relationships. The foundation relationship is resting in the hand of God, trusting God for the provision of our lives, and in that provision walking in obedience. That is salvation, the good relationship which produces good feelings. Nothing else can endure.

---

70 *The Hound of Heaven*, Francis Thompson, from *The College Survey of English Literature*, ed., A. M. Witherspoon. Harcourt, Brace, & Co., New York, 1952. p. 1162-4.

The role of sexual imagery in Scripture is a
stunning picture of intimacy and inclusiveness between God and His people. In the negative sexual
images it is also a frightening picture of exclusion and of the bareness of life without God, as in
various references to Israel's adultery and har-
lotry, or in the image of Hosea and Gomer, or Babylon the harlot in the Book of Revelation.

But God has already made His choice, we are all
called to be not of this world but of Him. The
choice then remains with us. We can drink of the
world's perennial well of pansexualism, or we can
drink of the well of God who stands outside the
world calling us to Himself for our true fulfillment and place in life to be made in His image,
male and female.

Epilogue

The Bad News and the Good News

We have hovered for the most part around the issues of sexual morality for the preceding three chapters. Other issues, however, are related to the matters of sex and gender which are also divisive within the Christian community. The matters of abortion, of inclusive language, and of the ordination of women to the priesthood and episcopate have to some degree arisen as matters of conflict out of a similar background in thinking. These three, with sexual morality issues, tend to have a common theme of hyper-individualism, autonomy, and challenge to established, in particular, Biblical, authority. The issues often arise over the expression of the women's liberation movement in a manner which appears to oppose masculine virtues in men but to wants to attribute them to women.

It would be unfair to suggest that those issues bear no kinship to a genuine Godly effort at uniting justice and mercy, or that there are no legitimate issues being raised. Nevertheless, there are sufficient similarities between the feminist position as often held and the characteristics of the "perennial philosophy" which has manifested itself in Kinseyan pansexualism to warrant an investigation beyond what we can do here.

The "unisex" theme, for example, which is fairly firmly associated with the positions of those who defend pro-choice abortion, support inclusive language, and work for the ordination of women to the priesthood and episcopate is often difficult to distinguish from the pansexualism of the previous chapter and would appear to have some of its roots therein. The tendency to confuse "sameness" with moral and spiritual "equality", to confuse submission to authority with oppression and lack of personal integrity, and the insistence that it makes little or no difference as to who (male or female) does what, all suggest an underlying pattern similar to that of pansexualism and the perennial philosophy. The tendency for extreme feminists to turn to pagan mother goddess religion only confirms this suspicion.

The abortion issue, for Christians, hinges on the value one places on persons, and where one believes a fetus becomes a person. The inclusive language and the ordination issues hinge on the meaning of 'masculine' and 'feminine', on whether the "power and authority" image developed above is correct,[1] and on a Biblical understanding of human nature and the will of God for human nature.

Decisions made in these areas either by the Church or the government concerning abortion, women's ordination, and inclusive language need to be reviewed in the light of the opposition between the Biblical worldview and the perennial view of pansexualism. Unless one is doing strange things with the term 'Christian', one cannot make decisions based on a view hostile to the Bible and still legitimately claim that one is following the Christian way. It is always possible, of course, that there are reasons not associated with either the perennial philosophy or pansexualism which will still legitimately justify any of the debated conclusions and practices, and those will have to stand on their own merits.

If spiritual warfare consists first of all in loyalty to the truth, and the maintenance of an arena in which the Body of Christ can gather to share viewpoints and each "tell our story", and if the battle belongs to God, not us, then spiritual warfare does not end in winners and losers. For those seeking truth, who are glad therefore to give up their errors, it ends in the abundant life. It ends in the truth that sets us free. To that end, we can all say "amen!" to Socrates who urged his listeners to tell him when he was mistaken on a matter, for he did not want to be victim to falsehood. Socrates viewed truth as objective, and desired to find and live in it. Socrates was manifesting the philosophical version of the discipleship of the cross, the willingness to die to one's own view in order to get at reality, in our present case, the will of God.

The expulsion from the Garden of Eden ends with the scene of the cherubim being placed at the east of the Garden, "and a flaming sword which turned every way, to guard the way to the tree of life" (Genesis 3:24). It is natural, given the immediate context, to assume that the sword was put there to

---

1 See above, *Inclusion and Exclusion*, "Sex and Gender in Creation".

179

prevent Adam and Eve from returning and eating from the tree of life. But I believe, put into the wider context of the meaning of Scripture, that sword is none other than the Sword of the Spirit, the word of truth, and that it was put there to guard, that is, protect, the way to the Tree of Life so that should Adam and Eve ever repent and want to return, they might be able to do so. It was put there to keep the way open, not closed. The word of truth is to keep the sign posts to the Tree of Life properly pointed, and not allow Satan to confuse the directions. The Sword will not permit the world, the flesh, or the devil to take over truth or to dominate the arena of truth sharing. It is a promise of redemption, not damnation. The way to the Tree of Life is by the word of truth, which Adam and Eve had violated in listening to the serpent, the father of lies. In their fallen state, they could see truth only as threat and retribution, not promise, and so God would one day have personally to intervene to convey to them the deeper meaning of His purpose and will, and restore their willingness to live in truth, "in the light", as St. John urges (I John 1).

The question is often asked, "Well, who would presume to know the will of God?" as though such a presumption were the height of arrogance. If we can presume to understand moral and spiritual truth at all, we can presume to know the will of God. And if God presumes to speak His will to us, the presumption and perhaps arrogance is on the other side, to claim that we cannot know the will of God, or that God is not able to speak clearly enough for us to hear. If God has spoken, then humility lies then in obedience to, not in postured ignorance of, His will.

A friend who has done workshops in churches around the country in the United States and Canada commented to me about the amount of fear that he found among born-again and Spirit-filled Christians. I suggested to him that some of that fear is caused by Christians being caught between on one hand the expectations of their faith to march out in confidance and on the other hand the underlying fear that secular science really does have the last word. That is to say, we have not resolved the alleged conflict between religion and science, and so we have a niggling suspicion beneath all our religious faith that our religion is pitted against truth. Christians often therefore feel that they

are being asked to walk on water when they "know
perfectly well" that the water will not hold them
up.

Our deepest failure, in my estimation, has been
our lack of faith, our lack of openness to the
truth, our fear that God will not come through when
put to the test of practical reality. The result
has been an essentially powerless Church in a secular society. We have hidden instead behind the
shield of infallibility, but exhibited little ability to make a difference in the affairs of the
world. We have been afraid to "test the spirits"
to see whether they are of God. If we are not
engaged in constant reality testing, we will inevitably set ourselves up for failure.

But reality testing means asking, "How do you
know?" of any assertion or claim on our beliefs,
and especially on our own inner claims that we
would want others to share with us. We are afraid
because we have had it drummed into our heads that
science has somehow "disproved" the Bible or the
Christian faith or the existence of God, etc. Our
ineptitude at reality testing has been one of the
primary causes of the divisions in the Church. We
were seldom willing, even among ourselves, to put
our beliefs to the test of open inspection, we were
not willing to listen to the voices of others who
had criticisms of our stand sufficiently to honestly know whether they might be right.

Witness the debacle of the reformation period.
Luther may have been right, but his followers were
unwilling or unable to persist in the Church and
trust the Spirit of God to carry their witness to
truth to the heart of the Church. As a result, the
reformation and counter-reformation both became
more "counter" than "reformation". It has not
often been pointed out that the beginning of the
ecumenical healing of the broken Church over the
last century has been abetted far more than hurt by
the scientific study of the Bible. It is just beginning to be understood that science arose in only
one culture in human history, at the end of a mil-

lenia of saturation by the Biblical worldview, and was philosophically a product of that view, not a rebellion against it. [2]

I have stood firmly on the principle that the Church does not have its agenda defined by the world, that it has an objective truth to share. Now I want also just as firmly to affirm the other side of that coin. The practical application of our faith in God is for Christians of differing persuasions to have an arena within which these different viewpoints can be shared, no matter how objectionable they may seem or indeed be. Listening to a contrary viewpoint in love does not imply the acceptance of that viewpoint, nor does it imply the inability of the Church to take a stand on what it believes. But to refuse even to listen with compassion may hinder God from speaking His word to the Church in a given situation, and will certainly block our relation and witness to that person. It is only in our trusting, first, that all truth is of God, even the bits that non-believers discovered first, and, secondly, that Christians must gather openly to share what they believe God is giving them of the truth, that the whole picture of truth can emerge. We need to be able to stand on our ground, but we also need to be able to become vulnerable to the point of honest and gracious and compassionate listening to one another.

In any gathering of conflicting views, there will inevitably be, in this fallen world, hidden currents of pain and felt rejection. There will be a fear that "I will be rejected because my view is unacceptable". The Christian arena must convey to the participants, "You are acceptable as a person, no matter what anyone thinks of your viewpoint. You are our brother/sister, and we are willing to lay down our lives for you." That sense that I am valuable apart from my viewpoint frees me to let go of my viewpoint sufficiently to look honestly for the truth. I can "be me" even if my viewpoint turns out to be wrong. That is our freedom in Christ.

---

2 See Stanley Jaki, *Science and Creation*, Scottish Academic Press, Edinburgh, 1974. Also my work, available in the summer of 1988, *Personality, Empiricism, and God*, for the philosophical case to show that science cannot operate without presupposing the Biblical notion of a personal God. See endnote on Emmaus Ministries.

These are both books requiring some philosophical background. There are many lighter materials also available.

But it is a freedom that comes only through the testing of it in sometimes painful reality. We need to experience that kind of acceptance. We need to experience that vulnerability through speaking the truth as we see it, listening to the truth as others see it, and seeing what truth in fact emerges as we mutually listen for the voice of God to draw us into unity. The power of conviction that comes out of such a process arises out of the objectivity of the presence of God in such a gathering. Our freedom to let go and look for objective truth beyond ourselves gives God the freedom to give us that objective truth.

And is it not clear that that is exactly what legitimate and Godly science tries to do in its own appropriate realms? If we cannot find the truth in that manner, then we are forever condemned to trying mutually to brainwash one another, for reasoned discussion will be an impossibility. And that is the same as saying that there is no objective truth, and that the Kingdom is an illusion.

The liberal in our midst will tend to reach out for new directions, and in doing so will often flirt with the secular world where interesting things are happening. He will in doing so occasionally fall into secular patterns and paradigms. But the liberal may be the one who will hear what the Lord is saying to us that perhaps the world hears better than the church, as God used Cyrus the Mede to free Israel from Babylon. Secular persons have occasionally been involved in good projects ahead of Christians, as would seem to be the case in environmental concerns, civil rights, wholistic medicine, concerns for peace, etc. Christians in an age where Christianity is "legal", tend to get comfortable and therefore "conservative" for the wrong reasons, so God goes to the pagan who is listening, even if unaware that it is God to whom he is listening. We need the liberal to listen for us in that manner.

The conservative will want to hold onto the tried and true, but sometimes so strongly that he will stifle the new thing that God is about. God does not contradict Himself, and will not invalidate the revelation He has given us in Scripture and especially in the Incarnate life of Jesus. But that very revelation may have developments of which we were at one time unaware, as we now see clearly in the matter of slavery, and as we are being forced to grapple with in the matter of a just distribution of economic goods and a just economic system. Were there liberals in the Christian camp whom we refused to heed, so that God gave us over to the plague of communism? Did not Karl Marx hear a word from God, albeit in a distorted because secularized way, that the Church refused to hear?

It is when conservative and liberal, high church and low church, evangelical and charismatic, can let go of their intellectual agendas sufficiently to love the other person whether or not he agrees, it is when I get beyond the initial clash of opinions to hear a soul speaking, that there is another child of God over there, a warm body, a living being, who experiences pain and loneliness, who experiences joy and exaltation, and who would like to share with me the abundant life in Christ, that God can begin to reveal and to build the Kingdom with persons, not just ideas. It is then that we become committed to staying in the dialogue. There is someone over there too precious to walk out on. It is that kind of commitment, not only to God, but to each other, that God can use most powerfully to heal and reunite His Church.

It is out of my love for that other person that I *will* speak the truth to him as I see it. I *will* offer my perspective to be stirred into the pot, but likewise I will allow his perspective. Then as we discuss and reason about our experience of the issues, submitting ourselves logically and rationally and compassionately to the truth and listening for the voice of God, God will reveal Himself in glory and majesty. We will experience His presence and the Kingdom among us.

The "bad news" is that the world is fallen and hovering on the brink of self-destuction on more than one front. One wonders what to say in the face of the calamities that we face. I have maintained that spiritual warfare begins with preserving the arena of truth seeking and truth sharing. But it does not end there. We clearly are faced with more than flesh and blood, we are faced with principalities and powers, the sort of which most of us have little knowledge. The enormity of the evil in our midst cannot be explained by merely human ignorance, failure, or sin. And the Church is confused and divided nearly to the point of total ineffectiveness. But although God has called the Church into being, although the work of ministry is entrusted into human hands, God never urged us to put our trust in the Church or human hands.

The "good news" is that God Himself continues to redeem the world, and that He has not allowed belief in Himself to be contrary to truth, but that as we pursue the truth and as we trust to the witness that He has given of Himself, and share that witness with any and all around us, He will both redeem our sexual natures and prove His own case in a manner that will be clear and evident.

God does allow Himself to be tested. We cannot put God into a crucible, shake Him up with other chemicals and watch the results. But, if we ourselves get into the crucible of life with Him, which is surely where He is calling us into discipleship, and if we there allow ourselves to be shaken up with Him in open and honest confrontation with Himself and one another, the evidence (what else is revelation?) will pour out in clarity and abundance in ways that will satisfy the mind, the will, and the emotions. God will draw us to Himself. We will in the process lose our fear and apprehension about the reality of the world and of God, and of ourselves. And the issues of sexual morality and other matters around which we conflict at the present time will become truth, clarity, and abundant life.

Endnote

EMMAUS MINISTRIES

Other items by the Rev. Earle Fox relating to sexuality and the spiritual life:

A THEOLOGY OF HETERO-SEXUALITY - 12 cassette tape album providing a comprehensive foundation for a Biblical understanding of our maleness and femaleness made in the image of God. Cost: $45.80 plus $1.50 postage. Titles include:

1. Pagan/Secular View - Human Nature, Psychology, and the Cosmos.
2. Biblical View - ditto.
3. Man and Woman in the Image of God
4. The Sacrament of Selfhood
5. The Geography of the Soul
6. The Expanding Circle of Mother and the Search for Father
7. Nature - God's Womb for the Soul
8. The Inner Marriage
9. Healing the Sacrament of Marriage
10. Sexual Symbolism
11. Pornography and the Healing of Sexual Imagery
12. Sex Roles in the Body of Christ

SEX AND GENDER IN THE CHURCH, -- four articles bound in a set (approx. 50 pp.), will be available in the late spring of 1988. Cost, $1.75 @ (10+ copies $1.50 @) + postage $.90 (add $.25 for each additional copy). Includes:

1. "Gender, Sex, and Priesthood"
2. "Sexuality, Gender, and Renewal"
3. "Is Love an Adequate Guide?"
4. "A Case for Christian Chastity"

YAHWEH OR THE GREAT MOTHER? - MAN AND WOMAN IN THE IMAGE OF GOD - developing the Biblical case for a full scale psychology. Available summer, 1988.

GENDER, SEX, AND THE PLUMB LINE, (tentative title expected late summer, 1988), a look at the sex-ed philosophy and its effect of *Learning About Sex,* a current secular sex education textbook, by Gary F. Kelly, *Sexuality - a Divine Gift,* the sex education material sponsored by the Episcopal Church, and two others programs designed specifically to present a Biblical viewpoint on sexuality.

*   *   *   *

The following books will also become available during 1988:

BIBLICAL INNER HEALING (sub-title - *WHO WILL LET GENE OUT?*) -- putting secure Biblical foundations under emotional healing; available May, 1988.

PERSONALITY, EMPIRICISM, AND GOD -- the philosophical case for the Biblical roots of science. Fall 1988.

Summaries or tables of contents will be sent upon request.

For further information about other items dealing with a Biblical psychology and therapy, or to be put on the newsletter mailing list, write to:

> Emmaus Ministries
> 25 Parallel St.   or call - (203) 846-6892
> Norwalk, Ct. 06850

See back cover for further information on the Rev. Earle Fox and on Emmaus Ministries.

Further copies of *Biblical Sexuality and the Battle for Science* may be obtained from the above address at $5.95 @ - (5+ copies $5.45 @).

Inquire for prices on bulk quantities and dealer discount. Very favorable bulk rates in cases where free distribution to Church leaders is intended.

(Add $1.00 postage for the first copy, $.25 for each additional copy to the same address.)

REPORT OF THE TASK FORCE ON CHANGING PATTERNS
OF SEXUALITY AND FAMILY LIFE

Prepared at the Request of the 111th Convention
of the Diocese of Newark
By: The Task Force on Changing Patterns
of Sexuality and Family Life

The Rev. Dr. Nelson S. T. Thayer, Chair

The Rev. Cynthia Black

Ms. Ella Dubose

The Rev. Abigail Hamilton

The Rev. Dr. David Hamilton

Ms. Diane Holland

Mr. Thomas Kebba

Mr. Townsend Lucas

Dr. Teresa Marciano

The Rev. Gerard Pisani

The Rev. Gerald Riley

Ms. Sara Sobol

The Rev. Walter Sobol

* * * *

INTRODUCTION

Following the mandate of the Diocesan Convention on January, 1985, the Task Force on changing Patterns of Sexuality and Family Life has been meeting for study and discussion, focusing its attention on three groups of persons representative of some of the changing patterns of sexuality and family life: 1) young people who choose to live together without being married; 2) older persons who choose not to marry or who may be divorced or widowed; 3) homosexual couples. All three kinds of relationships are widely represented in the Diocese Newark, and it has been recognized that the Church's understanding of and ministry among the people involved has not been adequate.

The aim of the Task Force has not been original social scientific research. Members of the Task Force have engaged in Biblical, theological, historical, sociological and psychological study, and in extensive discussion of the issues raised. The intent of the Task Force has been two-fold: to prepare a document that would help the clergy and laity of the dioceses to think about the issues, and to suggest broad guidelines for the Church's pastoral response to persons in the three groups and to those not in those groups but who are concerned about the issues raised.

The process of study and discussion engaged the members at the deepest levels of their self-understanding as human beings and as Christians. We sometimes found ourselves confused, angry, hurt, uncertain. The subject brought up basic fears and prejudices which members had to struggle with corporately and privately. We become more deeply aware of our own fallibility and of our need for each other's response, correction and support. Each member is a distinct person with her or his own distinct experience and viewpoint; complete uniformity was neither sought nor attained.

But the Task Force became and remains convinced that such a process of search and person-to-person engagement is essential for the Church to respond to the social, cultural and personal realities involved in the changing patterns of sexuality and family life. Appropriate response to these issues requires the willingness to confront within ourselves some of our most deeply formed impulses and assumptions, and some of our tradition's most firmly embedded attitudes. This can only occur in a context of conversation with others whose experience and viewpoints enable our own to be transformed.

We understand the Church to be a community in search, not a community in perfection. As a community in search, the Church must recognize the needs among its members, among all Christians, indeed among all persons, for loving support, for mutual trust, and for growth through learning from each other. As one contemporary writer has put it "...as such a community the Church is of prime significance in making love a reality in human life - incarnating the Incarnate Love... These images affirm not only intimacy and mutuality but also inclusiveness; there are implications for a diversity of sexual patterns within a congregation. Different sexual lifestyles being lived out with integrity and in Christianly humanizing ways need not simply be tolerated -- they can be positively supported. The 'family of God' can ill afford to make the nuclear family its sole model." (James Nelson, *Embodiment*. Minneapolis: Augsberg Publishing House, 1978, p. 260.)

This report crystallizes the Task Force's perspective on these issues. It does not summarize each discussion, nor does it present all the research and data that informed these discussions. The report is offered to the Diocese of Newark to stimulate our corporate thinking and discussion. The Task Force's major recommendation is that discussion continue on an intentional, Diocese-wide basis. This and other recommendations are offered in the final section.

I. THE CULTURAL SITUATION.

The social and cultural changes that have occurred in American society over the past half-century are increasingly being reflected in the changing attitudes of members of the Anglican communion regarding some of the basic moral values and assumptions which have long been taken for granted. Profound changes have occurred in our understanding and practices in areas involving sexuality and family life. Traditionally, the Church has provided, virtually unchallenged, direction and guidance on these matters that deeply affect

the individual, the family unit and the community at large.
Today, the Church is no longer the single arbiter in these
matters, which were once thought to be within its sacred
province. Some of the factors that have led to the diminu-
tion of this status are:

1. Secularization of American society as it moved from a
predominately rural background at the turn of the century to
today's predominately urban setting. This has produced new
and competing centers of values and morality.

2. Social, economic and geographic mobility that has individually and collectively loosened structures traditionally
provided by the community, church and family. These structures tended to channel and constrict values, choices, and
behavior in the areas involving sexuality, marriage and family life.

3. Advances of technology, which have provided means of
disease control and birth control, which have effectively
separated the act of sexual intercourse from procreation.

4. Reduction of the age at which puberty begins. This
confronts children with issues of sexuality earlier than in
the past.

5. Adolesent dating without chaperonage. This removes a
powerful external structure of control of sexual behavior.

6. Many in contemporary culture begin and establish a
career at a later age than formerly. Marriage also tends to
occur later. These two developments combined with convenient
methods of birth control, the earlier onset of puberty and
the absence of chaperonage, significantly lengthens the period when sexuality will be expressed outside of marriage.

7. The gradual, but perceptible changes in attitude regarding what constitutes a "complete" human being: the human
body and sex are no longer considered something to be ashamed
of, and these physical realities as well as intellect and
spirituality constitute essential elements in the development
of a complete human being.

8. The decline of exclusive male economic hegemony, which
has resulted in a realignment of the male/female relationships
in society.

9. The existence of a better educated society, which does
not depend upon authorities to determine "what is right" on
issues such as nuclear war or power plants, abortion, birth
control, poverty, environment, etc.

10. The intensifying clash between the claims of traditional authority as demanded by the family, church and society and the aims of twentieth century men and women to seek
their own fulfillment in ways that were not necessarily acceptable in the past. This is, of course, an ancient ten-

sion; it gains its particular contemporary character in American society from the dissolution of the degree of ethical consensus as the society has become increasingly pluralistic.

The Church needs to think clearly about these social, cultural, and ethical realities. It must order its teachings and corporate life so as to guide and sustain all persons whose lives are touched by these realities. The challenges that these realities pose to our beliefs and practices must be examined and responded to.

As indicated in the introduction, this report is intended to contribute to the Church's understanding of these issues, and to offer perspective on and suggestions for the Church's response.

II. Biblical and Theological Considerations.

A. Tradition and Interpretation

The Judeo-Christian tradition is a tradition precisely because, in every historical and social circumstance, the thinking faithful have brought to bear their best interpretation of the current realities in correlation with their interpretation of the tradition as they have inherited it. Thus, truth in the Judeo-Christian tradition is a dynamic process to be discerned and formulated rather than a static structure to be received.

The Bible is misunderstood and misused when approached as a book of moral prescriptions directly applicable to all moral dilemmas. Rather, the Bible is the record of the response to the word of God addressed to Israel and to the Church throughout centuries of changing social, historical, and cultural conditions. The Faithful responded within the realities of their particular situation, guided by the direction of previous revelation, but not captive to it.

The text must always be understood in context: first in the historical context of the particular Biblical situation and then in our own particular social and historical context. The word of God addresses us through scripture. It is not freeze-dried in prepackaged moral prescriptions, but is actively calling for faithful response within the realities of our particular time. Any particular prescription in scripture, any teaching of the law, must be evaluated according to the overarching direction of the Bible's witness to God, culminating in the grace of Christ.

B. The Centrality of Christ and the Realm of God.

The central point of reference for the thinking Christian is the life, ministry, death, and resurrection of Jesus Christ. The history of interpretations of the meaning of that event begins in scripture itself and continues into our immediate present. The central fact about Jesus's life and teaching is that he manifested in his relationships, acts, and words, the imminent and future Kingdom of God, which will be referred to as the Realm of God.

The Realm of God as presented by Jesus in his relation- ships and in his parables is characterized by loving action on behalf of all men and women including especially the poor, the sick, the weak, the oppressed and the despised, the out- cast, and those on the margins of life. The Realm of God presents us with both the fulfillment and the transcendence of the inherited law. The Realm of God presents us with an overturning -- even a reversal - of the structures by which humans attempt to establish their own righteousness, which inevitably oppresses or exploits, or marginalizes others.

The challenge to the Church to respond creatively to changing patterns of sexuality and family live in America must be seen as an instance of the Holy Spirit leading us to respond to the blessing and claim of the Realm of God fore- shadowed and made continually present by the life of Christ Jesus. In his death Jesus exemplifies sacrificial love that is faithful to his vision of the Realm of God. In the resur- rection we know God's ultimate faithfulness and sovereignty.

It is in response to this central example and teaching of Jesus regarding the Realm of God that we attempt to discern what should be the Church's response to changing patterns of sexuality and family life. We discover in the actions and parables of Jesus that the Realm of God manifests grace un- fettered by legalistic obligation to tradition and "the law." When the choice is between observance of the law or active, inclusive love, Jesus embodies and teaches love. It is in the light of this fundamental principle of God's active rec- onciling love that any religious law or dogma, social or economic arrangement is to be assessed.

C. The Realm of God and Human Social Structures

The specific instances of changing patterns of sexuality and family life that this Task Force addresses do not occur in a cultural vacuum but in the cultural turmoil marked by the ten developments noted in the opening section of this document. Not one of these developments is morally unambigu- ous. All of them are marked -- as has been every development of social history -- by the human propensity for self-decep- tion and self-aggrandizement at the expense of others, which Christians call "sin."

Jesus's radical claim is that in his person the Realm of God confronts us, in every age, with out bondage to sin. Included in sin's manifestations are the social norms and arrangements by which we conventionally order our lives. In parable after parable Jesus presents us with the need to see historical relativity, the need to examine the arbitrariness and the maintenance of power by traditionals structures. The

Church itself and the authority of its traditional teachings is subject to judgement by the ongoing activity of the Realm of God.

Judged by the grace of God starkly presented by the parables, Jesus's preaching and his actions show us that response to the Realm of God requires us to be ready to perceive and modify those structures in our society that hurt and alienate rather than heal and extend love to those in circumstances different from our own.

With this consciousness we hear the challenges to our conventional attitudes and practices regarding sexuality and the family and try to discern how these challenges should influence our understanding of our traditional values and our response to new realities. We engage in this process knowing (and discovering anew) that all our thoughts are laced with our desire for self-justifiction, our need for self-aggrandizement, and the willingness to hurt those whom we see as opposing us. Sin is our human condition; it permeates all our institutions, all our traditions, and all our relationships, so it has always been for humankind; so it has always been in the Church.

D. Historical Relativity

Recalling our sinful condition causes us to look critically both at the Church's conventions and at the demands for change put forward by various groups in our culture. The relativizing impact of the Realm of God enables us to see more clearly what Biblical and historical research discloses: that beliefs and practices surrounding marriage and sexuality have varied according to time, culture and necessity. We tend to sacralize the familiar and project into the past our current practices and beliefs and the rationales supporting them.

Such is the case with our assumptions about marriage. We tend to project into early Biblical times a twentieth century model of monogamous self-chosen marriage when clearly, at various periods in the Old Testament records, polygamy was assumed (at least for the wealthy). Even into the Middle Ages a marriage was an economic event, perhaps an alliance, between two families or clans.

Marriage was not given the status of a sacrament by the Church until 1439. And not until 1563 did the Church require the presence of a priest at the event. And even then marriage functioned to solemnize an agreement which had been entered into more for reasons of procreation, the channeling of sexuality, and economic benefit to the families than as a means for preexisting love between the two persons to develop and flourish, as we expect of present-day marriage.

In the Bible and in our own Western heritage, sexuality outside of marriage has been proscribed for women--not men. When women were found adulterous, the violation was of property rights rather than of sexual morality as we tend to conceive it, because women were viewed as property of fathers, and then of their husbands.

Homosexual behavior was condemned because it was part of pagan religious practices from which Israel sought always to differentiate itself. Biblical scholarship maintains that in the story of Sodam and Gomorrah, Lot's concern was not with the homosexual nature of implied rape of his guests, but with such behavior as a violation of rules of hospitality. Homosexuality as a fundamental human orientation is not addressed in scripture; and Jesus himself was entirely silent in the subject.

E. Revised Understanding of the Person.

A major change in perspective is occuring in religious thinking regarding sexuality and the body. Greek philosophical and agnostic thought had great influence on the early development of Christianity. Since that time the Church has tended to teach that the body is a dangerous vessel, subject to temptation and sin which temporarily houses the superior soul or spirit. Whereas the Greeks regarded the mind or spirit as able to reach its triumph only by freeing itself from the corrupting captivity of the physical body, the Hebrews knew no such separation. In Hebraic thought one does not _have_ a body, one _is_ a body. What we today refer to as body, mind, and spirit were -- in Hebraic thought -- dimensions of an indivisible unity.

The contemporary more Hebraic understanding of the person runs counter to the traditional dualistic teaching of the Church, which has tended either to try to ignore the fact that humans are embodied selves, or has looked at the physical, sexual body as the root of sin. The contemporary attitude views sexuality as more than genital sex having as its purpose procreation, physical pleasure and release of tension. Sexuality includes sex, but it is a more comprehensive concept.

Sexuality is not simply a matter of behavior. Our sexuality goes to the heart of our identity as persons. Our self-understanding, our experience of ourselves as male or female, our ways of experiencing and relating to others, are all reflective of our being as sexual persons.

We do not have _bodies_, we _are_ bodies, and the doctrine of the Incarnation reminds us that God comes to us and we know God in the flesh. We come to know God through our experience of other embodied selves. Thus our sexual identity and behavior are means for our experience and knowledge of God. This theological perspective means that issues of homosexuality, divorce, and sexual relations between unmarried persons involve not only matters of ethics but have to do with how persons know and experience God.

It is our conclusion that by suppressing our sexuality and by condemning all sex which occurs outside of traditional marriage, the Church has thereby obstructed a vitally important means for persons to know and celebrate their relatedness to God. The teachings of the Church have tended to make us embarrassed about rather than grateful for our bodies. As means of communion with other persons our bodies sacramentally become means of communion with God.

III. Ethical Essentials.

From the perspective of Jesus's teaching regarding the Realm of God, all heterosexual and homosexual relationships are subject to the same criteria of ethical assessment -- the degree to which the persons and relationships reflect mutuality, love and justice. The Task Force does not in any way advocate or condone promiscuous behavior which by its very definition exploits the other for one's own aggrandizement. The commitment to mutuality, love and justice which marks our ideal picture of heterosexual unions is also the ideal for homosexuals unions. Those who would say homosexuality by its very nature precludes such commitment must face the fact that such unions do in fact occur, have occurred and will continue to occur. The Church must decide how to respond to such unions.

It is becoming clear that many persons -- single, divorced, or widowed -- may not seek long-term unions, while some commit themselves to such unions without being formally married. The overriding issue is not the formality of the social/legal arrangement, or even a scriptural formula, but the quality of the relationship in terms of our understanding of the ethical and moral direction pointed to by Jesus in the symbol of the Realm of God.

The challenge to the Church is to discern and support the marks of the Realm of God in all these relationships. The Church should be that community above all which is marked by its inclusion of persons who are seeking to grow in their capacity for love and justice in their relationships and in their relation to their world-neighbors. The Church should actively work against those social and economic arrangements which militate against the establishment of such relationships.

IV. Marriage and Alternate Forms of Relationship

Our nation has been described as a "highly nuptial" civilization. This means that for whatever reasons many Americans see marriage as a vehicle for happiness and satisfaction. Life-long marriage offers the possibility of profound intimacy, mutuality, personal development, and self-fulfillment throughout the years of the life cycle. On the other hand, of course, a marriage can be marked with the sin of self-centeredness and exploitation of the other, and by the estrangements of male from female, weaker from stronger.

Ideally, marriage can be a context in which children can develop their identities by drawing on both male and female ways of being a person. It can therefore provide a uniquely rich context for the formation of children into adults who cherish and intend the qualities of the Realm of God --love and justice -- in the context of ongoing relationships marked by sacrifice, forgiveness, joy, and reconciliation. It can also give to parents the opportunity to mature and develop their own capacities for caring generativity.

The Church must continue to sustain persons in the fulfillment of traditional marriage relationships both for the well-being of the marriage partners and because such marriage provides the most stable institution that we have known for the nurturing and protection of children. But the Church must also recognize that fully intended marriage vows are fraught with risks. Belief that deeper knowledge each of each in marriage will enable the original intentions of love and devotion is not always fulfilled. Persons living through the dissolution of marriage need especially at that time the support of an understanding and inclusive community. Such is true obviously also for divorced persons, whether living singly or in new relationships.

One of the Church's present deficiencies is its exclusionary posture toward those who have "failed" in the conventional arrangement of marriage and family and the conventional understanding (and avoidance) of sexuality has blinded us to present reality. The Church needs actively to include separating and divorced individuals and single parents.

The Church must take seriously that Jesus's teaching and manifesting of the Realm of God were concerned not with the formal arrangements of our lives but with our responsiveness to the vision of the Realm of God. Admittedly, this confronts all of us with a relativization of all personal, social and economic arrangements by which we live. We cannot live without structure in our relationships; but these structures are subject to continual correction by the image of the Realm of God. If the Church is to err it must err on the side of inclusiveness rather than exclusiveness.

Marriage has served as a stabilizing force in American society, channeling sexuality in socially acceptable directions, providing a structure for the procreation and nurturing of children, and enabling enduring companionship between a man and a woman by defining the legal and spiritual responsibilities of the married couple. Although marriage has taken many forms in human society, it has been a central, constant building block of human society in all cultures. The power of sexuality both to attract persons, and satisfy persons, and to disrupt the social order has been recognized in the practices, mythologies, and laws of all cultures.

Marriage has bound the family, clan, and tribe to customs and traditions which insure survival and identification of a people as a people. The church must consider the consequences of calling into question institutional relationships which have permitted the Church to flourish and survive. However, our contemporary consciousness of racial, sexual, and economic domination and exploitation has raised our culture's consciousness about some of the oppressive, repressive and exploitative dimensions of marriage and family arrangements. This heightened sensitivity, combined with a cultural ethos that favors self-fulfillment over the dutiful but self-abnegating adherence to conventional marriage and family arrangements has caused many to deny that life-long monogamous, heterosexual marriage is the sole legitimate structure for the satisfaction of our human need for sexuality and intimacy.

There are those who think that even though the forms have been enormously diverse, the pervasive human tendency to union with an individual of the opposite sex in a committed relationship and the universal presence of family structure in some form evidences something fundamental about the nature of the created human order itself. Biologically, this has been the only option for the perpetuation of the human race as we know it. While other arrangements may be appropriate to the given nature of particular individuals, monogamous, life-long marriage and family organization ought not to be thereby relativized as simply one option among others.

Given the Church's traditional view of the exclusive primacy of marriage and the nuclear family and the (relative) opprobrium with which the Church has viewed other options, the Church must learn how to continue to affirm the conventional without denigrating alternative sexual and family arrangements. Again, the criteria are the quality of the relationships and their potential for developing persons responsive to the Realm of God. The Church must find ways genuinely to affirm persons as they faithfully and responsibly choose and live out other modes of relationship.

We live after the Fall. The metaphor of the Realm of God reinforces the realization of brokenness and finitude in all our human arrangements and relationships. We sin daily in our self-deception, self-centeredness, self-justification, and readiness to exploit and oppress others for our own material and emotional self-aggrandizement. And this is clearly seen in our readiness to interpret scripture and tradition to reinforce what we perceive as our own best interests so that we appear righteous and those who differ from us appear unrighteous.

The dynamic process of God's incarnational truth has brought us to a time in history when the critical consciousness made possible by modern forms of knowledge - including Biblical scholarship - enables us to see the Realm of God as a present reality relativizing all human knowledge and social arrangements. We are therefore suspicious of the invocation of tradition even while we believe that in God's ongoing creation not all relational arrangements are equally aligned with a caring God's purposes for humankind.

Those who believe that the heterosexual family unit headed by monogamous heterosexual partners offers the best possibility for the development of children who will become confident, loving, compassionate and creative adults must acknowledge the historical fallibility of the family in accomplishing such results. All sexual and family arrangements must be judged by the same criteria suggested by the metaphor of the Realm of God.

Ultimately, do couples (of whatever orientation) and families of (whatever constitution) exist for the sake of their own self-fulfillment? The Gospel does not support such an individualistic possibility. Nor does it support promiscuous behavior, which by its very nature uses the other person simply for one's self-aggrandizement, whether mere sexual release, as compensation for feelings of inadequacy or to express hostility. Theologically, patterns of sexual and family arrangements are to be judged according to the degree to which they reflect and contribute to the realizeation of the Realm of God. Since this is a dynamic not a static reality, continual diversity, exploitation, experimentation, and discernment will mark the life of the faithful Church.

In the absence of set rules, great demands are thus placed on clergy and others who counsel persons regarding these issues. We believe that at the level of congregational life, the Church ought not focus its concern on this or that particular pattern. The Church's focus ought to be on persons as they seek to understand and order their lives and relatinships. All relationships and arrangements are to be assessed in terms of their capacity to manifest marks of the Realm of

God: healing, reconciliation, compassion, mutuality, concern
for others both within and beyond one's immediate circle of
intimacy.

V.   Considerations Regarding The Three Alternate Patterns

As indicated in the Introduction, the Task Force decided
to address specifically the Church's response to young adults
who choose to live together unmarried, adults who never married or who are "post-marriage", due to divorce or the death
of their spouse, and homosexual couples. We do not address
the subject of adolescent sexuality, although we agree on the
need for more thorough-going education of adolescents within
the Church regarding sexuality and relationships.

We believe that certain questions of context are appropriate whenever persons consider beginning a sexual relationships: a) Will the relationship strengthen the pair for
greater discipleship in the wider context? Will they be better enabled to love others? Will their relationship be a
beneficial influence on those around them? b) Will the needs
and values of others in the larger context be recognized and
respected, especially the needs of their own children (if
any), their parents, and their parish community? Since an
ongoing sexual relationship between two persons occurs within
a network of relationships to parents, children (perhaps
adult children), colleagues, and fellow parishioners, such a
relationship needs to be conducted with sensitivity to the
possible emotional and relational effects on these other persons.   c) What is the couple's intention regarding the procreation and/or raising of children?

Regarding the relationship itself, the following consider-
ations are appropriate: a) The relationship should be
life-enhancing for both partners and exploitative of neither.
b) The relationship should be grounded in sexual fidelity and
not involve promiscuity.   c) The relationship should be
founded on love and valued for the strengthening, joy, support and benefit of the couple and those to whom they are
related.

A.   Young Adults.

One of the issues facing the Church in our time comes
under the broad category of what used to be called "pre-marital sex." The issue for the Church to which attention is
given in the following discussion is specifically defined as
that of young adults of the opposite sex living together and
in a sexual relationship without ecclesiastical or civil ceremony. (Of course, many young adults, for economic and social reasons share housing without having a sexual relationship. We do not address these relationships in what follows.)

From an historical perspective, such relationships are not
unfamiliar to our culture. For many years common-law marriage had legal validity for purposes of property and inheri-
tance settlements. Attitudes concerning careers, emotional
and sexual commitments and intimacy, marital economics, and
experiences (either through observation or background) all
contribute to decisions concerning the form of relationship a
man and a woman choose. In the contemporary world, young
adults may live together to deepen their relationships, as a
trial period prior to a commitment to marriage, or as a
temporary or a permanent alternative to marriage.

In order to maintain the sacredness of the marital relationship in the sacrament of Holy Matrimony, The Church has
generally been opposed to the actions of couples choosing to
live together without ecclesiastical or civil ceremony. Opposition has been and is expressed both in direct statement
and by silent tolerance. The effect of the opposition has
been to separate those couples from the ministry of the
Church, to the detriment of the quality of their relationship, of the spiritual growth of the individuals, of their
involvement in the mutual ministry of the Church, of their
contribution to the building up of the Christian community.
Current research documents that persons living under these
circumstances are less likely to profess an affiliation with
an established religion or to attend church. And yet these
persons might well benefit from a church affiliation.

To minister to or engage in ministry with those who choose
to live together without marriage does not denigrate the
institution of marriage and life-long commitments. Rather it
is an effort to recognize and support those who choose, by
virtue of the circumstances of their lives, not to marry but
to live in alternative relationships enabling growth and
love.

In a community in search, all benefit from mutual support
and concern. Although living among persons of differing
lifestyles can be threatening, it can provide those who have
committed themselves to a lifelong relationship in marriage
the opportunity to renew, to reform, to recreate their loyalties and vows in an atmosphere of alternative possibilities.

We emphasize that the Church's focus should be on persons
as they seek to understand and order their lives and relationships. All relationships are to be assessed in terms of
their capacity to manifest marks of the Realm of God: healing, reconciliation, compassion, mutuality, concern for others both within and beyond one's immediate circle of intimacy. Extending the image of the Church as a community of
persons in search raises pastoral implications. A community
in search seeks wisdom, understanding and truth in the expe-

rience and hopes of each of its members and from those (too often ignored) who choose not to participate in that community.

Both at the diocesan and congregational levels, the Church can actively engage in education and discussion on all issues of sexuality. Members of the congregation, persons from specific disciplines in the secular world, and persons who have in their own lives wrestled with pertinent issues can all be asked to participate in such efforts. Congregations should encourage open, caring conversation, leading to trust and mutual, supportive acceptance. This makes more credible the Church's claim to faithfulness to the Realm of God.

Persons who have been ignored or rejected by the Church's ministry, or who have assumed such rejection, can only be reached and loved by a community that witness in _deed_ to its faith that God calls all people to new hopes, to new possibilities, by a community that knows it does not have all the answers and in which each member contributes to its growth and future wholeness in the Realm of God.

B.   "Post-Married" Adults

Some mature persons, by life-long choice or because of divorce or the death of a spouse find themselves unmarried but desiring an intimate relationship. We affirm that there can be life-enhancing meaning and value for some adult single persons in sexual relationships other than marriage. Economic realities may militate against traditional marriage arrangements. For example Social Security payments are reduced for two individuals who marry; channeling inheritances for children can become legally expensive and complicated where re-marriage occurs; maintaining a one-person household is for many persons prohibitively costly.

The choice of celibacy or estrangement from the Church for such persons who choose not to marry is not consonant with the Church's hope of wholeness for all persons in the Realm of God. Our understanding of the Church is one of inclusiveness. As we struggle to understand what the Church is called to in our time, one of our goals is inclusion in the Christian body of persons who have thoughtfully chosen lifestyles different from that of the mainstream.

Because we are whole human beings, and not, in the last analysis, separate compartments of body and soul, therefore the spiritual, mental, emotional, physical, and sexual aspects of our personalities are all to be nurtured and expressed in responsible ways if we are to continue to grow towards wholeness in our mature years. We are created sexual beings, and our spiritual health, no less than any other aspect of health, is therefore linked to sexuality. When therefore, mature single adults choose to celebrate their love and live their lives together outside of marriage, provided that they have considered and responded sensitively to the public and personal issues involved, we believe that their decision will indeed be blessed by God and can be affirmed as morally acceptable and responsible by the Church.

C.   Homosexual Couples.

Changing patterns of sexuality and family life confront pastors and congregations with new challenges and opportunities for understanding and for ministry. Rather than arguing about these issues we need first to listen to the experience of those who are most directly involved. Where homosexuality is concerned, fear, rejection, and avoidance by the heterosexual community is common and entrenched; we believe that pastors and congregations must meet members of the homosexual community person to person. The first step toward understanding and ministry is listening.

We need as much as is possible to bracket our judgements and listen to persons as they are. The Church needs to acknowledge that its historic tendency to view homosexual persons as homosexual rather than as persons has intensified the suffering of this 5%-10% of our population. A congregation's willingness to listen is a first step toward redeeming our homophobic past.

Listening is also a first step toward acknowledging that our own understanding needs ministry. Those of us fearful and angry regarding homosexuality need liberation, and this can only come through person to person communication. So the Church's response includes permitting itself to be ministered to by the homosexual community.

This process will help the Church recognize that whatever our historical experience, we encounter each other as we are with all our many limitations and potentialities. What we may become is a function of our open meeting of each other and of the reconciling, empowering spirit of God active in such open meeting.

Such person to person meeting, by means of open forums, small group discussions, and one to one conversations needs to be accompanied by the study of Biblical, historical, theological, and social scientific perspectives. Accurate information and informed opinion are important counterbalances to the fear and distortion, which have so often inhibited the Church's ability to respond appropriately.

Listening opens the door of hospitality, which has so long been firmly shut. Such words as ministry and hospitality, however, still suggest a relationship of inequality, we and they. As such they perpetuate the image of the Church as separate from the homosexual community. In fact, however, we believe that the Church should be as inclusive of homosexual persons as it is of heterosexual persons. In this light, all the normal avenues of inclusions should be available to homosexual persons.

Criteria for membership, for participation in church committees, choirs, education, vestries, etc. and for ordination should be no different for any given group. Some persons express fear that including homosexual persons in the full round of church life will influence others - especially children - to become homosexual. In fact, we know of no evidence or experience to confirm that such association can bring about a homosexual orientation.

Ideally, homosexual couples would find within the community of the congregation the same recognition and affirmation which nurtures and sustains heterosexual couples in their relationship, including, where appropriate, liturgies which recognize and bless such relationships.

VI. Recommendations

Sexuality is an integral part of our God-given humanity. The Church must devote more attention to sexuality in its child, adolescent, and adult educational programming. As we understand more about the nature and meaning of our sexuality we will learn how to respond more appropriately to persons of many different circumstances.

Change in the Church's life is an ongoing process. We therefore urge education and discussion at all levels of diocesan life.

Specifically we recommend the following:

1. That all collegial groups such as the Commission on Ministry, the Newark Clergy Association, and all other regular commissions and committees of the diocese address these issues as they impact their areas of responsibility and concern.

2. That the March/April Clergy day, 1987, and the June, 1987 Religious Education Conference include sexuality among the issues to be considered.

3. That Congregations develop programs appropriate to their setting and circumstances which enable education and discussion regarding issues of sexuality and the Church's response to changing patterns of sexuality and family life. In addition to providing structured educational programs, the Church should be a community where persons can discuss their experience and clarify their self-understanding relationships and courses of action. We would urge congregations to provide space and time, for example, for parent groups whose children are gay or lesbian and who want to discuss the

implication of this for their own lives. Likewise, gay and lesbian couples may want to meet with each other or non-gays for support and friendship.

4. That Convocations support and perhaps sponsor such programs as suggested above.

5. That a group similar to this Task Force be established to facilitate discussions at the congregational level, to monitor the process, and to report to the diocesan Convention of 1988, perhaps with recommendations or resolutions.